ALL WHO Cₐ

A short, illustrated accoᴜ ᴀ the
Mountain Meadows Massacre

Terence Parker

ROMANS

Published in 2008 by:

ROMANS
24 King's Road
Salisbury
Wiltshire   SP1 3AD

A CIP catalogue record is available at the British Library.

ISBN 978-0-9554843-1-5
10   0-9554843-1-6

Printed in England by:

SALISBURY PRINTING
Greencroft Street
Salisbury
Wiltshire   SP1 1JF

Source material has been acknowledged, as has the origin of each illustration and quotation except where the origin is unknown. Where the origin is in doubt, credit has been afforded to the most likely original source. Most quotations and illustrations are from the nineteenth century but licences were sought when this seemed appropriate. Notwithstanding this, any person who believes that a significant infringement of rights has occurred is invited to contact the publisher.

Dedication

This book is dedicated to the memory of three little girls: **Rebecca Dunlap (6), Louisa Dunlap (4), and Sarah Dunlap (1)**, who, on 11 September 1857, suffered the most appalling misfortune but stuck together and helped each other to survive. Their simple humanity shines out brightly from several eye-witness accounts of the dark, horrific massacre at Mountain Meadows.

The trio's conduct speaks well of their parents, Jesse and Mary Dunlap, who perished on that dreadful day, along with their seven brothers and sisters.

The three little girls grew up, married and two had children. Despite her partial blindness and an arm withered during the massacre, Sarah married Captain Lynch, the army officer who had brought the children back to Arkansas two years after the massacre; Sarah was 37 and Lynch 75.

(Facts recounted in a *Fort Smith Elevator* article dated 20 Aug 1897)

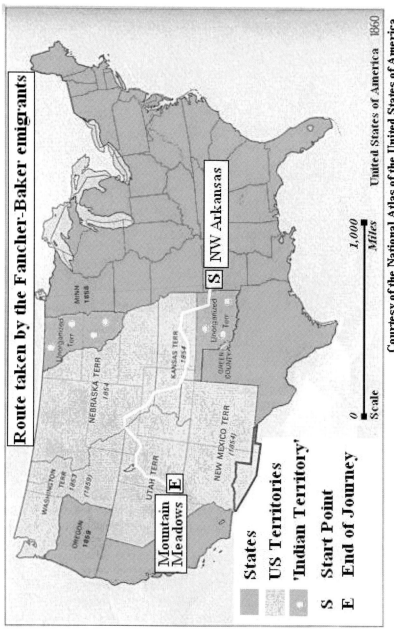

Route taken by the Fancher-Baker emigrants

S NW Arkansas

Mountain Meadows

E

States
US Territories
'Indian Territory'
S Start Point
E End of Journey

Scale
0
1,000
Miles

United States of America 1860

Courtesy of the National Atlas of the United States of America

Preface

All who are old enough to talk must be 'put out of the way'.

Mormon decision in Iron County, Utah, after the
Arkansas emigrants had seen a white attacker.

In September 1857, a party of emigrants camped beside a spring on a flat pasture in Utah, known as Mountain Meadows. Within days of their arrival, their wagon train - which included about 140 men, women and children - was attacked; within a week, all except seventeen of the youngest children were dead. Those killed were unarmed and each of the men had been struck down simultaneously, not by the Indians present, but by a Mormon militiaman whose leader had, moments earlier, agreed to protect the emigrants from harm.

The Mountain Meadows Massacre took place on 11 September 1857. Until the Oklahoma bombing in 1995, it was the largest mass murder of United States citizens; even after '9/11' 2001, it remains the third largest.

All Who Can Tell presents a concise, chronological account of the massacre, based on the most illuminating eyewitness accounts. It also views the world as a whole, in order to expose the strong, underlying cause of the massacre. The story is one of conflict, courage and controversy. The conflict is over; the courageous lie silent beneath the meadowland; but the controversy has yet to be resolved.

3 March 2008   Terence Parker
Salisbury, England

Baker family wreath at the 1999 Memorial on 26 September 2007.

The labels have been given a digital overlay to clarify the names of
individual family members who died, and of the children
who survived (the three lowest labels).

Contents

*A **profile of the author** appears after the epilogue.*

Maps and Illustrations

Abbreviations:

NAUSA   *Courtesy of the National Archives ,United States of America.*
LDS   *Courtesy of the Church of Jesus Christ of Latter-day Saints.*
MMMMonFdn *Mountain Meadows Massacre Monument Foundation.*
TOP   *Taken by the author or (IMP) by his wife.*

Extract from the verso page Page (II) of this book:

Source material has been acknowledged, as has the origin of each illustration and quotation except where the origin is unknown. Where the origin is in doubt, credit has been afforded to the most likely original source. Most quotations and illustrations are from the nineteenth century but licences were sought when this seemed appropriate. Notwithstanding this, any person who believes that a significant infringement of rights has occurred is invited to contact the publisher.

IX

MOUNTAIN MEADOWS viewed from the 1990 (overlook) Memorial

1. INTRODUCTION

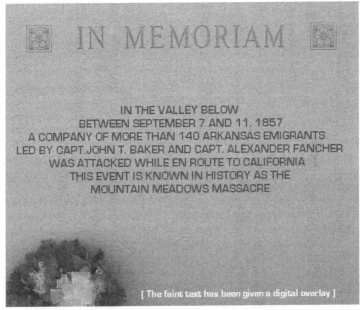

IN MEMORIAM

IN THE VALLEY BELOW
BETWEEN SEPTEMBER 7 AND 11, 1857
A COMPANY OF MORE THAN 140 ARKANSAS EMIGRANTS
LED BY CAPT. JOHN T. BAKER AND CAPT. ALEXANDER FANCHER
WAS ATTACKED WHILE EN ROUTE TO CALIFORNIA
THIS EVENT IS KNOWN IN HISTORY AS THE
MOUNTAIN MEADOWS MASSACRE

[The faint text has been given a digital overlay]

Illustration 1a   The 1990 (overlook) Memorial: main inscription.   *TOP*
The names of the emigrants who died and the children who survived were inscribed
on this memorial 133 years after the massacre occurred. The list is incomplete.

Life on America's Utah frontier during the 1850s was hard. The aftermath of an attack on James Wright and his family in 1859 clearly illustrates this:

"The wagons were turned from the road, the ground being covered with feathers from bedding, and fragments of clothing. Under a wagon, with a crippled babe in her arms, lay Mrs James Wright with a serious wound in her back; and inside the wagon, half delirious and exhausted by loss of blood, Mr James Wright lay mortally wounded. The poor sufferers were

attended by a little son five years of age, who supplied their feverish lips with water, and also brought them the sorrowful news that all their companions were either killed or had fled."

This grim report is one of many in a file given to US President Buchanan after Congress had become aware of the Mountain Meadows Massacre. The scale of the massacre belittled all earlier and subsequent wagon train attacks, including the attack on the Wright family, but today - in the twenty-first century - few people have heard of Mountain Meadows.

I had not heard of Mountain Meadows, myself, until I bought *The Salt Lake Tribune* on 9 September, 2007, while I was holidaying in Utah. There were several articles devoted to the massacre: one described the event, another reviewed its legacy, and yet another outlined the ceremonies due to take place on 11 September 2007 – the 150th Anniversary.

As I paid for the paper, I asked the sales assistant if it contained international news: I was assured it did – both north and south Utah were covered! Her reply was not strictly correct: the *Tribune* does have snippets of world news, but the 'world' of most small-town Americans is their own state. This might explain why many of my American friends have not heard of the massacre, even though it is as historically important as *Custer's Last Stand* in 1876. There is - however - more to it than isolation.

A very heroic *last stand* occurred at Mountain Meadows but - to the still lingering embarrassment of Mormon Utah - heroism was surpassed by treachery, when the disarmed male defenders were murdered by white settler militiamen. Consequently, publicity has always been discouraged, but - as the 150th anniversary approached - a surge of publicity was inevitable.

The date of the massacre - 1857 - intrigued me. On the 26 September, 2007, I found myself standing in Mountain

Meadows gazing around. It was a moving experience: so much so, that I decided to produce this book. I say produce - rather than write - because many of the most revealing paragraphs were written by two people who stood in the meadows long before me: Brevet Major James Henry Carleton of the US Army; and John Doyle Lee, who was a major in the Utah Militia, a bishop of the Mormon Church and an Indian farmer[1].

Illustration 1b   The main contributors to my story.   *NAUSA* /johndlee.net

Carleton arrived at the massacre site with his soldiers and federal officials, in May 1859 – almost two years after the massacre - but he was determined to find out what had happened. The answers Carleton prized out of the local settlers and Indians enabled him to produce a hazy, but surprisingly accurate picture [2] of the massacre. This picture was chillingly clarified by John D Lee in his confessions [3], in May 1877 – almost two decades after the massacre. Lee finished writing these confessions a few days before he sat on a coffin in Mountain Meadows, to await the arrival of four US Army bullets [4].

Fortunately, and much to my surprise, I was able to obtain a copy of *The Mountain Meadows Massacre* by Juanita Brooks [5] from an English bookshop. It proved most helpful, as did the *National Archives of the United States of America (NAUSA)*. Material was drawn, too, from the libraries of Utah and other states, and the archives of the *Church of Jesus Christ of Latter Day Saints (LDS)*.

The myriad links of the Mountain Meadows Monument Foundation [6], Mountain Meadows Association [7] and John D Lee [8] websites led me to the additional information I needed to present this story. I have also had brief, encouraging email contact with Burr Fancher and Cheri Baker Walker: descendants of the two principal families involved. Last but not least, I have benefited from the passage of time: most contemporary reports and illustrations are in the public domain.

Thousands of words have been written about the massacre and at least one other book is in production. Consequently, the sequence of the massacre is, by now, well established but - and it is a big but - why did deeply religious white settlers participate so willingly in the cold-blooded murder of unarmed, white emigrant men, women and children? One of the plaques on the hilltop memorial overlooking the site notes rather plaintively: "(that) the exact causes and circumstances that fostered the sad events which ensued over the next five days at Mountain Meadows still defy any *clear and simple explanation*". (Author's italics)

In this book I set out to do two things: firstly, to present a short, chronological, well illustrated account of the massacre based upon the most illuminating eye-witness accounts; secondly, to offer a *clear and simple explanation* of the powerful underlying cause of the Mountain Meadows Massacre.

4

Why am I able to do this? Firstly, because I am a keen student of individual violence, revolution and war. Secondly, because my own childhood experience [9] helps me to assess the recollections of the child survivors. Thirdly, because I am able to compare the Mountain Meadows Massacre to a very similar massacre which occurred at Cawnpore, in India, during the summer of 1857 [10].

* * *

Computer buffs may wish to zoom into Mountain Meadows on *Google Earth.* The search engine will not do this for you, but by tracing up from *Central, Utah,* to *Enterprise, Utah,* you can find Mountain Meadows, just left of the main road (Utah 18). When you have the correct location, you will see a small square: click on the square to view a 'pop up' photograph of the memorial cairn. There may also be a second 'pop-up'.

Most books about the massacre do not look at the world as a whole. This is a serious omission. We humans are like the ants scurrying about the Utah desert; the only difference is that we scurry about the world. When sunlight strikes the desert, all the ants respond in the same way; when the sun's continually varying radiation strikes our world, we humans are affected - all around the globe. There will be more about this in a later section, but let us look, first, at the year 1857.

Notes and references:

1. Indian farmer: a person appointed and paid to encourage local Indians to farm rather than attack white men.

2. Carleton's Report. *Special Report of the Mountain Meadow Massacre* by J H Carleton, Brevet Major, United States Army, Captain First Dragoons – written in camp at Mountain Meadows, Utah Territory, on May 25th 1859.

3. Lee's confessions. John D Lee's confessions* were presented through - and subsequently published by - his attorney: William W Bishop. Lee finished his confessions at Pioche, Nevada, on May 17th, 1877.
(* *Mormonism Unveiled or the Life and Confession of John D Lee*), published in 1877, in St Louis.)

4. Utah's firing squad employed five riflemen – one with a blank to ensure anonymity. Utah ceased using firing squads in 2004.

5. Juanita Brooks. *The Mountain Meadows Massacre*, Paperback edition, University of Oklahoma Press, 1991.

6. http://1857massacre.com
7. http://www.mtn-meadows-assoc.com
8. http://www.johndlee.net

9. I was born in India: a country where horrific religious massacres occur frequently, even today. Cawnpore is within a day's drive of my birthplace.
At the age of seven, I was uprooted from India (dusty, sunny and bright) and made the long journey to London (food rationing, very cold, with bomb-shattered streets everywhere) to stay with unfamiliar, war-weary but loving relatives.
My earliest childhood memories are of rifle shots (which killed dogs next to my primary school); grief (over the rabies death of a neighbour's child) and gravestones (which my father often photographed, in my presence, so that a picture of the grave could be sent to relatives in England). The memories are morbid and mild, but relevant to this story.

10. *Wheeler's Entrenchment* in **Cawnpore (Kanpur), India, in June 1857.** There was a siege followed by a surrender/safe passage offer, but treachery led to death of all the men, and some women/children. Finally, the remaining women and children were killed to stop them revealing the treachery. (More about this in Sections 13 and 14 of the book.)

2. 1857

Illustration 2   The financial panic of 1857.   *Book illustration, c1858*

The year 1857 may be likened to the crest of a wave, not of water, but of human emotion: a wave whose influence stretched around the globe. The upsurge of that wave would, soon afterwards, set populations against each other in a series of great wars: the American Civil War; a more devastating civil war in China; and even two Maori Wars in New Zealand.

As the year opened, many individuals were buoyed up high by the surf of that wave: financial speculators; excited moral campaigners; and a cleansing phalanx of firebrand clerics. In India, the new chaplain [1] of the Red Fort in Delhi was guiding a succession of fervent, but narrow minded Christian missionaries into the heart of Hindu/Moslem/Sikh India just as equally fervent, Islamic radicals were flowing in from Afghanistan. In America, Brigham Young, President of the Mormon Church was driving forward his *Reformation* [2] to fire up the faithful and gather in the strays.

* * *

The growing instability of American society was already evident [3] in April 1857, as the ill-fated settlers prepared to leave Arkansas. New York was mired in scandal: police corruption had reached an untenable level and insidious dishonesty was beginning to destroy America's financial system. The effects reverberated all the way to California.

In May 1857, the US Supreme Court ordered disbandment of the corrupt New York Municipal Police and its replacement by a new force: the Metropolitan Force. The Municipal Force refused to disband; a police/police battle ensued. During the chaos which followed, gang warfare and street robbery escalated as policeman fought policeman over who had the right to arrest a particular suspect. This extremely violent period was graphically portrayed in the 2002 film *Gangs of New York.*

As the year progressed, the ills of society became even more apparent. On 24 August 1857, embezzlement of railway bonds caused the New York Branch of the Ohio Life Insurance and Trust Company to fail, leaving a mountain of debt. Panic followed: major stocks fell 10% overnight, and fortunes were lost. Depositors demanded payment in gold to protect themselves but, on 12 September 1857, disaster struck: the steam ship *SS Central America,* laden with fifteen tons of federal gold destined for the eastern banks, sank in an unusually violent storm near South Carolina. On 3 October, there was a run on the banks; by the 13 October, the banks were forced to close; they did not reopen until November. In the meantime, businesses collapsed. Others slowed almost to a standstill and a prolonged period of depression followed until the outbreak of the Civil War. The slave-fuelled economy of the South was less affected; this increased the confidence of the slave-owning states.

Financial uncertainty spawned social unrest; both urban and rural communities suffered violence. While public order was breaking down in New York, violent arguments over slavery troubled rural communities, even those remote from the institution, and such arguments became entangled with religion.

*　　*　　*

In April 1857, life in India appeared calm and peaceful. The employees of the British East India Company [1] continued their exotic, perfumed existence amid a magnificent diorama of splendid military uniforms; plump, bejewelled maharajas; and leaner, occasionally more sullen, lower caste Indians. By the end of May 1857, many of those East India Company employees would be dead; very many more would die in the months which followed.

*　　*　　*

Before, during and after this turmoil, America's population continued to drift westward toward the Pacific coast, attracted by the promise of land and a succession of 'mineral rushes'. California entered the Union in 1850; in 1852, Californian mines yielded $81M in gold. Collapse of the banks, and the value of paper money, sent people rushing off to dig or migrate or both.

Migration was dangerous: Indians had always posed a threat; but, in 1857, the emigrants who passed through Utah found themselves embroiled in a white man's war. Utah's Mormon governor, Brigham Young, had decided to defy the President of the United States of America.

* * *

It was through such controversy that the Fancher [4] and Baker wagon trains slowly trundled, accompanied - it was rumoured - by a group of roughnecks known ominously as the 'Missouri Wildcats' [5]: roughnecks who delighted in riling Mormons.

Notes and references:

1. *Christians in India* and the *British East India Company* are explained in Appendix A to Section 13 of this book.

2. *Reformation*: this was a spiritual rejuvenation, very like Mao Tse Tung's Chinese *Cultural Revolution* in the 1960s.

3. US scenario in 1857. Main source: Gregory J Christiano *www.urbanography.com/1857*

4. Train Names: My understanding is that - prior to their joint departure from Salt Lake City - the Fancher and Baker trains had travelled separately from Arkansas, after departing on different dates.

5. Juanita Brooks (Page 219) mentions the 'Missouri Wildcats'; she reiterates the Mormon view that they were a group of aggressive, boastful ruffians. Others deny the very existence of 'Missouri Wildcats'. The truth probably falls somewhere between these two impressions. The issue is considered on Pages 38 and 39 of this book.

3. SAINTS

Illustration 3a   Joseph Smith Jr.   *Lucian Foster, c1843*
Founder of the Mormon Church.

The Church of Christ - the original name of the Mormon Church - was founded by Joseph Smith in Fayette, New York, on 6 April 1830. Smith declared himself the recipient of a divine revelation from the former inhabitants of America. It came in the form of golden plates, each inscribed in an ancient language. He translated the plates with the help of the *Angel Moroni*, and their content became the basis of the *Book of Mormon*. Joseph Smith was, himself, ordained by the angel. After a further revelation in 1838, he renamed his organization

11

The Church of Jesus Christ of Latter-day Saints. Throughout this book, I refer to it as the Mormon Church, and to its members as Mormons. It was the custom of Mormons to refer to other persons as either saints (Mormons) or gentiles (non-Mormons).

Gentile, to some, is an irritating term, implying, as it does, exclusion or lesser status. This did little to endear the early Mormons to their fellow Americans, many of whom adhered strictly to one of the long established forms of Christianity. Neither did the zeal of the Mormon's missionaries, some of whom successfully combined conversion with the acquisition of yet another *plural wife.* It was one such incident, which would influence the Mormon Church's attitude to the Fancher-Baker Train.

Illustration 3b   Parley P Pratt   *LDS*
A charismatic polygamist.

The prominent Mormon charismatic, Parley P Pratt, took as <u>his</u> ninth wife, the wife of Hector McLean, a San Francisco custom-house official. McLean's wife eventually fled east with their two children. Enraged but unable to legally retrieve his wife and children, McLean pursued Pratt and murdered him near Van Buren [1] in northwest Arkansas. This happened on 13 May 1857 – just as the Fancher-Baker emigrants were leaving the same area. McLean was a Californian, but he committed the murder in 'Fancher-Baker' country. Despite McLean's Californian origin, the Mormon Church seemed to conclude [2] that the Fancher-Baker emigrants played some part in Pratt's murder.

As one would expect, the polygamy concession – the outcome of yet another divine revelation – drew the Mormon Church into conflict with both territorial and federal authorities. Furthermore, the Mormons' tendency - once they were in positions of power - to favour saints over gentiles caused resentment.

During the twenty-seven years between its birth in 1830 and the Mountain Meadows Massacre of 1857, the Mormon Church suffered almost continuous, often extremely violent persecution. From its birthplace in New York, the main body of the church was driven in turn through Ohio, Missouri and Illinois, to its final resting place in the Utah desert.

On 27 October, 1838, Missouri Governor Lilburn W. Boggs signed a military order directing that the Mormons be driven from his state or exterminated. In the same month eighteen Mormons - including at least one small child - were killed by a mob at Haun's Mill, Missouri. Illinois proved even less hospitable: the church's founder, Joseph Smith, and his brother were murdered by yet another mob in 1844, while they were imprisoned in Carthage, Illinois.

At the end of the 1846-48, Mexican-American War, Utah became a US Territory [3], with Brigham Young – Joseph Smith's successor – as the territory's first governor. While this formalised the status quo, members of the Mormon Church still viewed themselves as a persecuted minority who had been unjustly hounded out of the more congenial eastern states. Indeed, many Mormons saw themselves as separate from American gentiles whom they regarded increasingly as the enemy; and the feeling was mutual.

In mid-1857, Brigham Young ejected several allegedly corrupt federal employees. The latter complained vociferously. Some vote-seeking politicians amplified their complaints until, eventually, President Buchanan decided to remove Young from his governorship. In May 1857, President Buchanan appointed Alfred Cumming, a non-Mormon, to be Governor of Utah. The President also appointed a number of non-Mormons to other Utah administrative and judicial positions. In order to protect these federal appointees and uphold law and order, Buchanan authorised Colonel Albert Sydney Johnston and 2,500 federal troops to accompany the officials to Utah.

The officials were unable to complete their takeover. Mormon raiders destroyed the federal army's supplies and stampeded the army's horses and cattle. Furthermore, by burning the Utah grasslands, they forced Johnston's men to spend a harsh winter at Fort Bridger, about 100 miles northeast of Utah's capital Salt Lake City. This very effective Mormon raid proved to be the only significant clash of the two armies, during the short, but chastening Utah (or Mormon) War.

Not surprisingly, given the strife and turmoil of those years, Utah Territory had its own militia, the Nauvoo [4] Legion, allied closely to the Mormon Church. Indeed, most militia officers held ecclesiastical appointments. There was also a third hierarchy, into which federal funds flowed: the Indian agencies. Some militia officers were bishops of the Mormon Church and Indian agents. To complicate matters even more, the close family or personal relationships which existed amongst the Mormon founders often overrode the formal lines of control.

Brigham Young
(displaced) Governor of Utah
(displaced) Superintendent of Indian Affairs
President of the Mormon Church

George A Smith
One of the twelve
Apostles of the
Mormon Church and
a message carrier for
the Church President

1857

Utah Military Hierarchy

Commander-in-Chief of the
Nauvoo Legion (the Utah militia)
General Daniel H Wells

Illustration 3c   Military policy makers and strategists.   *LDS*

The Mormon's military structure [5] is, perhaps, of most relevance to the massacre. As one would expect, **Governor Brigham Young** (deposed but still in post) was the de facto director of Utah's military operations in early September 1857. Below him, command passed (via **George A Smith**, one of the Twelve Apostles and 'father of southern Utah') through **General Daniel H Wells** (Commander-in-Chief of the territorial militia: the Nauvoo Legion), to **Colonel William Dame** (head of the Iron County Brigade) [6]. Mountain Meadows was situated in Iron County [7], a southern area of Utah Territory. A photograph of Dame appears in a later section of this book.

Illustration 3d   Paiute Indians in ceremonial dress.   JK Hillers, c1872

The Mormon Church espoused the abolitionist - anti-slavery - cause and treated Indians humanely, in contrast to the prevailing attitude of the 1850s: '*the only good Injun is a dead Injun*'. The Mormon Church viewed the Indians as valuable allies – particularly before and during the Utah War when they could call upon no other. Indeed, during the lead in to the Mountain Meadows Massacre, many Mormons viewed the Indians as *Jehovah's battleaxe*.

The Indians [8] who participated in the Mountain Meadows Massacre would seem, from all accounts, to have been a loose gathering of mainly Paiute Indians bands drawn from a broad swathe of Utah. In 1857, the many desert Indian tribes had barely emerged from the stone-age. They possessed few firearms (other than those they had acquired at Mountain

Meadows) and were, until then, reliant upon clubs, knives and the bow and arrow.

Notes and references:

1. Parley Parker Pratt's death: *Deseret News,* 1 July 1857.

2. Lee's Confessions.

3. Territories/States: Some more recent sources lack accuracy. My understanding of the territory/state situation along the Fancher-Baker wagon train route in 1857 is:

> **Arkansas** (Statehood 1836, but its 'territory'extended beyond the state's official borders);
> **California** (Statehood 1850);
> **Kansas** (still a Territory, until 1861);
> **Missouri** (Statehood 1821, but its 'territory' extended beyond the states official borders);
> **Nebraska** (still a Territory, until 1867);
> **Utah** (still a Territory, until 1896);
> I presume that the Indians still roamed free in **Indian (Unorganised) Territory**.

It seems that, if you used an Arkansas post-code, you were considered to be in Arkansas state or territory. Utah mail was cut off during the 'Utah War'.

4. Nauvoo was the idyllic city the Mormons briefly established in Illinois on a swampy bank of the Mississippi, before being driven off into the desert.

5. Militia Chain of Command Internet source: http://www.law.umkc.edu/faculty/projects/ftrials/mountainmeadows/commandc hain.html See also Note 6 below.

6. <u>Brigades/battalions/companies</u> Like the Boers, the Utah militia had few uniforms and a fluid, often unclear organisation tangled up with other ecclesiastical/administrative structures - all dominated by strong 'founder member' personalities.

7. <u>Mountain Meadows</u> was in Iron County (in the Iron Mountain area of Utah Territory) in 1857. Today, in the modern State of Utah, Mountain Meadows is in Washington County.

8. <u>Indians.</u> I usually use the word *Indians*, rather than quote a specific tribe (nation) because more than one tribe (nation) may have been involved in the massacre. The word 'nation' is appropriate today. For example: the Paiute Nation.

4. THE FANCHER-BAKER TRAIN

Illustration 4a   A settler's wagon at Pipe Spring National Monument.   *TOP*

It must be difficult for anyone who has not experienced the vastness of the United States, to fully appreciate the hazards facing wagon trains in the 1850s.

Unpredictable extremes of climate added to seemingly insurmountable obstacles: rivers which meandered, almost out of sight within deep, steep-sided canyons; and snow-capped mountain ranges which loomed, grey and forbidding, above

19

arid desert plains which often stretched from horizon to horizon. The journey from the northwest counties of Arkansas to California – a distance of over a thousand miles, even as the crow flies – was not something undertaken lightly: timing was crucial and only well-prepared wagon trains were likely to succeed.

Alexander Fancher sold 200 acres of land in Benton County, Arkansas, before setting out for California in April 1857, with his family and a large herd of cattle [1]. At about the same time, several other wagon trains left northeast Arkansas: the Baker's from Carroll County; the Huff's from Benton County; the Tackitt's from Washington County; the Cameron's and Miller's from Johnson County; and the Mitchell's and Dunlap's from Marion County. As each wagon train's journey progressed, there would have been periods of independent travel interspersed with train merger when danger threatened or when obstacle crossing required cooperation. Now and then, an individual might join a train for employment or protection, and leave when it suited him; others might join as a group. If disaster struck a train in a remote location, many of the victim's names might never be known.

By the 1850s, a network of trails had been established across North America. Some had been established by the Indians over centuries, and exploited by early Spanish and European explorers; others had been hewn during mineral exploitation; and the most recent linked river ferry drop-offs to the ever-expanding federal land grant areas. It was along such trails that the Fancher Train progressed at an average speed of about 10 to 15 miles per day. The train's route would have taken it along the *Arkansas Emigrant Road* (formerly the *Cherokee Trail*) which followed the Arkansas River through Kansas Territory and Nebraska Territory to the Platte River.

Doctor Brewer of the United States Army later reported to Brevet Major Carleton [2] that, on 11 June 1857 he had seen a train of about 40 wagons at *O'Fallon's Bluff* on the Platte River. It was referred to as 'Perkins' Train' after its leader at that time. However, the Doctor believed, from its size (about 40 heads of families, many married and single women, and many children) and one of its vehicles (a carriage of unusual construction, decorated with a stag's head) that it was the Fancher Train. He further stated that the train consisted of fine cattle stock and respectable people, who were well dressed, quiet, orderly and genteel. There were three carriages; several ladies rode in the 'stag's head' carriage, which the Doctor had observed closely as he rode along beside it. His fellow officer shared his opinion that this was one of the finest trains they had seen.

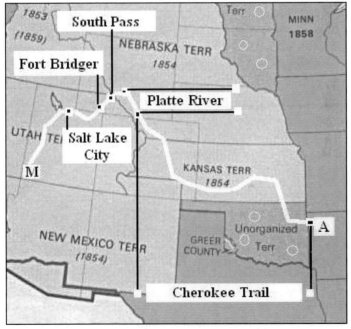

Illustration 4b   The route to Mountain Meadows from Arkansas.

Beyond the Platte River, the train would have headed north to the *Oregon Trail,* near *Independence Rock,* and then south into *South Pass:* the easiest passage through the Rockies. Beyond this pass lay *Fort Bridger,* where all routes into Utah Territory met the Oregon Trail. Fort Bridger was the privately-owned emigrant supply stop where federal troops languished after the Mormon raids. Mormon raiders burned the fort down a few months after the Fancher Train had passed through.

By early August 1857, the Fancher Train was resting 6 miles east of *Salt Lake City,* waiting for cooler weather before it crossed the Mojave Desert. The Fancher Train had hurried through Salt Lake City, after an inhospitable, sometimes hostile reception. Under strict orders from their church, Mormons refused to sell grain to emigrants; furthermore, the few services they did offer were outrageously overpriced.

By the time the **Fancher Train** left Salt Lake City, its number of wagons, cattle and emigrants had increased considerably. Amongst others, it gained the recently arrived **Baker Train** which had not left Carroll County until May. The **Fancher-Baker Train's** 30-50 well-laden wagons, several ornate carriages, oxen, horses and about 900 cattle made it one of the most valuable trains ever to leave Salt Lake City [3].

Beyond Salt Lake City lay two roads across the *Great Salt Lake Basin:* the n*orthern route* along the *Humboldt River,* or the s*outhern route* along the *Old Spanish Trail.* A slow train, with cattle, late in the season would avoid the northern route, in case the winter snows trapped them. Captain Alexander Fancher, who had led a train through the southern route in 1850, did the same in 1857. Other slightly faster trains, including older brother John Fancher's and the Scott's took the northern route. Melinda Scott's father, William Cameron, remained with the Fancher-Baker Train.

Illustration 4c (Opposite): The *Old Spanish Trail* in Southwest Utah.

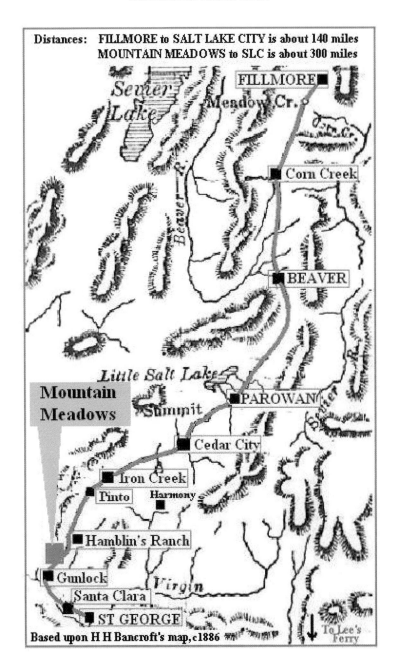

Distances: FILLMORE to SALT LAKE CITY is about 140 miles
MOUNTAIN MEADOWS to SLC is about 300 miles

FILLMORE

Sevier Lake

Meadow Cr.

Corn Creek

BEAVER

Little Salt Lake

Mountain Meadows

Summit

PAROWAN

Cedar City

Iron Creek

Pinto   Harmony

Hamblin's Ranch

Gunlock   Virgin

Santa Clara

ST GEORGE

To Lee's Ferry

Based upon H H Bancroft's map, c1886

Illustration 4d   The *Old Spanish Trail* at Mountain Meadows in 2007.   *TOP*

Travelling at about 10 miles per day, upon the increasingly difficult terrain, the Fancher-Baker Train followed the *Old Spanish Trail* - through Corn Creek, near Kanosh - to *Mountain Meadows*. A prominent Mormon, Joseph Hamblin, camped with the emigrants near Corn Creek, in early August 1857. Hamlin later described the train [2] to Brevet Major Carleton: *'emigrants, mainly from Arkansas; not over 30 wagons; several tents; 400/500 horned cattle; 25 horses and some mules'*. Hamblin also told Carleton that he had been on his way to Salt Lake City, and that he had advised the emigrants to rest by the spring at Mountain Meadows, some four miles from his summer residence. Hamblin described the emigrants as *'ordinary frontier, homespun, folk; with some rude, rough outsiders, calculated to get the ill will of the inhabitants* [2].*'* Hamblin also informed Carleton that the emigrants had poisoned a small spring at Corn Creek [4]; this had led to the death of several cattle and several Indians, whose kin were much enraged.

The emigrants arrived at Mountain Meadows, in family groups on the evening of Sunday, 6 September 1857. They set up camp a short distance from the spring which emerged beside the flat pastureland. (The spring has created a creek, which is out of picture, on the left, in Illustration 4d.) Cattle spread over the surrounding meadows which were overlooked by low hills on either side. Men and women probably went about their various tasks, as children tumbled out of the wagons and amused themselves in their new surroundings [5].

Notes and References:

1. Fancher-Baker Train: After reading many accounts of the form-up and journey of the Fancher-Baker Train, I have laced together the most credible sections of several accounts. Captain Fancher and Captain Baker gained their titles as the accepted/elected leaders of their respective wagon trains.

2. Carleton's Report.

3. Richness of the Fancher-Baker Train: Many reports and statements support this view. None seem to question it.

4. You may wish to be wary of Hamblin's statements, for reasons which become evident in later sections of this book.

5. **A Nominal Roll of the emigrants** has been added at Appendix A to this section.

Appendix A to Section 4

Nominal Roll of the Emigrants

Illustration 4e   An emigrant family, 1886.   *NAUSA (69-N-13606C)*

This family was not at Mountain Meadows, but it is fairly representative of the casualty lists which follow below. Each family may have had several covered wagons to accommodate themselves, their supplies and their belongings; and to offer shelter against the elements.

Unless otherwise indicated [1], the names in the LEFT HAND COLUMN of this appendix appear on the 1990 (overlook) Memorial, which lists all persons thought to be present when the Fancher-Baker Train rolled into Mountain Meadows on Sunday, 6 September 1857.

William A Aden	19	*Carleton's List* [5] *(in italics)*
John Beach	21	*naming the 15* surviving*
		children he interviewed:
John T Baker	52	
Abel Baker	19	
George W Baker	27	
Manerva A Beller Baker	25	
Mary Lovina	7	
Melissa A Beller (ward)	14	
David W Beller (ward)	12	
Martha Eliz (survivor)	5	*Betsy? (No 1*)*
Sarah Frances (survivor	3	*Frances? (No 2*)*
William Twitty (survivor)	9mths	*too young (No 3*)*
		to give a name
William Cameron	51	
Martha Cameron	51	
Tillman	24	
Isom	18	
Henry	16	
James	14	
Martha	11	
Larkin	8	
Nancy (Niece of WC)	12	
		Calvin (Cameron)? (No 4*)
Allen P Deshazo	20	
Jesse Dunlap	39	
Mary Wharton Dunlap	39	
Ellender	18	
Nancy M	16	
James D	14	
Lucinda	12	
Susannah	12	
Margerette	11	
Mary Ann	9	
Rebecca J (survivor)	6	*Rebecca (No 5*)*
Louisa (survivor)	4	*Louisa (No 6*)*
Sarah (survivor)	1	*Sarah (No 7*)*

27

Lorenzo Dow Dunlap		42	
Nancy Wharton Dunlap		42	
Thomas J		17	
John H		16	
Mary Ann		13	
Talitha Emaline		11	
Nancy		9	
America Jane		7	
Prudence Angeline	(survivor)	5	*Prudence Angelina (No 8*)*
Georgia Ann	(survivor)	18mths	*? ? Demurr? (No 9*)*

William M Eaton		?
Silas Edwards		?

Alexander Fancher		45	
Eliza Ingrum Fancher		32	
Hampton		19	
William		17	
Mary		15	
Thomas		14	
Martha		10	
Sarah C		8	
Margaret A		7	
Christopher Kit Carson	(survivor)	1	*Charles (No 10*)*
Triphenia D	(survivor)	22mths	*not mentioned by Carleton*

James M Fancher	25
Frances F Fancher	?
Robert Fancher	19

Saladia Ann Brown Huff		?	
(Peter Huff)	Not at MM – died en route from a spider bite.		
William		?	*William H Huff (No 11*)*
Elisha		?	
Son 1		?	
Son 2		?	
Nancy Saphrena	(survivor)	4	*Sophronia (No 12*)*

John Milum Jones	32

Eloah A Tackitt Jones		27	
Daughter 1		?	
Felix Marion	(survivor)	18mths	*not mentioned by Carleton*
Newton Jones		?	
Lawson McEntire [3]		21	
Josiah Joseph Miller		30	
Matilda Cameron Miller		?	
James William		9	
John Calvin	(survivor) [5]	6	
Mary	(survivor)	4	*Mary 1 ? (No 13*)*
Joseph	(survivor)	1	*Joseph 4 ? (No 14*)*
Joel D Mitchell [6]		23	
Charles R Mitchell [6]		25	
Sarah C Baker Mitchell		2?	
John		Infant	
John Prewit		20	
William Prewit		18	
Milum L Rush		28	
Charles Stallcup		25	
Pleasant Tackitt		25	
Armilda Miller Tackitt		22	
Emberson M (survivor) [5]		4	*Ambrose Mariam Tagit (No 15*)*
William	(survivor)	9mths	*not mentioned byCarleton*
Cynthia Tackitt		49	
Marian		20	
Sebrun		18	
Matilda		16	
James M		14	
Jones M		12	
Richard Wilson		?	

Solomon R Wood	20
William Wood	26

Not listed on Memorial

Mr Hamilton [1]   ?

Notes on the Nominal Roll:

1. 'Mr Hamilton' is mentioned in Lee's confessions, and other accounts of the massacre.

2. Number of child survivors: 17 are listed on the memorial; there may have been one more; we can never be sure.

3. Names often appear in phonetic *'frontier English'* (see, in some accounts 'Shirts' for 'Shurtz'). The Indian's *'pidgin English'* is even stranger: for example, 'Americats' or even 'Merry Cats' when they mean 'Americans'.

4. The total number present on 6 September, 1857, can never be accurately established. No proper head count of the dead was recorded by the Mormons after the massacre, but they thought that they buried 107 people [5]. By the time more caring persons arrived on site (US Army, May 1859), an accurate count was impossible. An estimate of 107+ seems reasonable; the train count with survivors would then be 124+.

5. Carleton's report. **Calvin** was 7 or 8 when he spoke to Brevet Major Carleton in May 1859. Calvin could not remember his surname, but said he **had two older brothers (Henry and James) and three sisters (Nancy, Mary and Martha)**; only a James is listed above under the Millers. Was Calvin a Cameron? A survivor (Joseph Miller?) claimed, after a year's separation, that **baby Mary was <u>his</u> sister**, but he didn't mention poor Calvin! One boy said 'I'm **William H Huff** '.

6. Two sons of Senator William C Mitchell. The senator demanded pursuit of the massacre perpetrators. He also met the child survivors when they returned to Arkansas.

5. JACK RABBITS AND QUAIL

Illustration 5   Mountain Meadows from the 1990 (overlook) Memorial.   *TOP*
(The wagons would eventually be 'corralled' near the author's added white flagpole.)

It seems clear that, when they arrived, the Fancher-Baker party felt safe at Mountain Meadows. There were no reports of immediate wagon encirclement, nor the appointment of outlying pickets. Indeed, the first rifle shot from an unidentified enemy seemed to catch them all by surprise. One of the surviving children later recalled that the emigrants were eating jack rabbits and quail when the shot knocked over a small boy, causing panic. Captain Fancher reacted quickly: he ordered half the men to engage the enemy with rifle fire, and the other half to circle and chain the wagons.

    Once this had been accomplished, earth defences were constructed: wagon wheels were lowered into shallow pits;

wagon bodies were filled with earth, and a shallow earth abutment/trench defence ring was created within the wagons. At the centre of the encircled wagons, a large pit was excavated to protect the women and children. To these defence works, one further excavation was added: one which revealed the main weakness of the emigrant's situation. Fifty years after the massacre, the writer Josiah Gibbs [1] discovered a partially excavated well that the emigrants had dug, just northeast of the central pit. Driven by the urgency of their task, and a desire to allow sufficient clear ground in front of the wagons, the emigrants had set up their circle some way away from their only water source: the spring.

It seems likely that the first attack occurred on the morning of Monday, 7 September: the day after the wagons rolled into Mountain Meadows. Reports suggest that - after a lethal first volley of rifle fire - several hundred Indians rushed at the emigrants between first light and sunrise, but were beaten off after they had killed seven emigrants and badly wounded others. Two Indian chiefs, too, were badly wounded, but the Indians managed to drive off, or kill, most of the emigrants' livestock.

Unknown to the emigrants, white men were involved in the attack, or had soon joined the Indians:

'I saw white men taking aim and shooting at the emigrants' wagons. They said they were doing it to keep in practice or to help pass off the time', John D Lee recalled [2]. *'One man, Alexander Wilden had placed a chair in the shade under a tree, over 400 yards from the emigrants; he continued to load and shoot, even though his weapon only fired a ball half the distance.'*

On the morning of Wednesday, 9 September, two emigrants were observed making a bucket run to the spring. Bullets flew around them but they got back safely. Later, a pair of emigrants braved the bullets to cut wood from nearby trees.

Sometime earlier, during the hours of darkness on Tuesday night, William Aden and another emigrant had slipped out to get help from Cedar City. On their way there, the pair had approached three Mormons, believing the trio would summon help to the train. William Aden [3] was immediately shot dead by one Mormon (William Stuart); his companion was wounded by a second Mormon (Joel White) but escaped back to the encircled wagons. He informed the shocked emigrants that Aden had been killed by a white man. Until then, only Indians had exposed themselves amongst the attackers, although it was later stated by eye witnesses that some of the 'Indians' were actually white men in disguise.

This was the moment of truth for both emigrants and Mormons. The emigrants realised that they were entirely on their own, surrounded by hostile Indians and belligerent, seemingly murderous Mormons. The Mormons realised that, if any of the emigrants old enough to talk reached California, the wrath of the East Coast would descend upon Utah. It was likely that they, the Mormons, would be crushed between the federal forces already assembled on their northern border, and an avenging army from California.

Within the wagon circle, the besieged emigrants grew increasingly weak through lack of water. Their wounded were beginning to die; their ammunition supply had dwindled to a few precious bullets and ball, but the Indians continued to harass them.

On the evening of Thursday, 10 September, not far away, the Iron County militiamen began to assemble in strength, as their officers heatedly debated the orders they had just received.

Notes and References:

1. *The Mountain Meadows Massacre.* Josiah F Gibbs, 1910.

2   <u>Carleton's report.</u>

3. <u>Lee's confessions.</u>

6. WHAT IS TO BE DONE ?

Illustration 6   Isaac C Haight   Utah SHS (CC ID # 20634)

While the Indians tried repeatedly but unsuccessfully to annihilate the emigrants, the Iron County militia officers wrestled with their dilemma and their consciences. They did this within the highly charged atmosphere of the day.

*   *   *

By September, 1857, Utah had adopted a siege economy within its areas of control, and a scorched earth policy between

Salt Lake City and Fort Bridger.

The American economy was in crisis; tangible assets and gold coin were in heavy demand; and every farmer and trader felt threatened. The emigrants passing through Utah consumed pasture, drank the precious water supplies and - now that trading with them had been forbidden - contributed little to Utah's economy. Furthermore, Mormons - still smarting from their earlier violent harassment - were being provoked by emigrants upset by the Mormon's refusal to trade. This uneasy Mormon/wagon train relationship greatly influenced events during the lead up to the massacre. The seriousness of this issue - the Mormon/wagon train relationship - may be gleaned from the following three perceptions of it:

The outsider's view: **The Remarks of Hon Stephen Arnold Douglas Delivered in the State House at Springfield, Illinois, on the 12th June, 1857 (and reported in the *Daily Missouri Republican* on 18 June, 1857)**:

"... the Mormon government, with Brigham Young at its head, is now forming alliances with Indian tribes in Utah and adjoining territories - stimulating the Indians to acts of hostility..(....some irrelevant text omitted...) – to prosecute a system of robbery and murders upon American citizens, who support the authority of the United States, and denounce the infamous and disgusting practices and institutions of the Mormon Government."

The official Mormon Church view (in response): **Editorial in *The Deseret* [1] *News*, No 26, Vol VII, Salt Lake City Wednesday, 2 September 1857:**

"That the citizens of Utah have formed alliances, as asserted by the Senator, is a lie too absurd to deserve even a denial, for

the citizens of Utah know their rights and duties too well to transcend their bounds, neither have they a desire or occasion for transcending them, either in this or any other matter.......
Therefore, on this point you are again, in your hot fury for office, found lying so grossly that you defeat yourself. When and where have Latter Day Saints, under any name, 'prosecuted a system of robbery and murders upon American citizens'? Never, and nowhere: on the contrary, they have ever striven for the just protection of the lives and rights of all, so far as is in their power..."

The unofficial Mormon Church view in Iron County: **John D Lee's recollections** [2] **from a meeting held in Cedar City on Sunday, 6 September 1857, just as the emigrants were beginning to arrive in Mountain Meadows:**

"About Sunday (6th [3]) of September, 1857, I went to Cedar City from my home at Harmony, by order of President Haight...."

(Isaac C Haight was then President of that 'Stake of Zion' – that is, the highest man in the Mormon priesthood in Iron County and, after William. H. Dame, in all of Southern Utah. As a Lieutenant Colonel in the militia, Haight was also Second-in-Command to Colonel Dame who commanded the Iron County Brigade.)

"..... He (Haight) said he wanted to have a long talk with me on private and particular business. We took some blankets and went over to the Old Ironworks, and lay there that night, so that we could talk in private and in safety. ....After we got to the ironworks, Haight told me all about the train of emigrants."

37

Author's Note: The offences which Haight ascribes to the emigrants are listed below together with the *author's thoughts* in italics:

a.   The emigrants were a rough and abusive set of men: *on the contrary, they were mostly families; but a few ruffians may have attached themselves to the train.*

b.   That they had, while travelling through Utah, been very abusive to all the Mormons they met: *this might apply to the ruffians, but was it really of any great significance?*

c.   That they had insulted, outraged, and ravished many of the Mormon women: *not very likely; their offences didn't make the Deseret News; some Mormon misbehaviour with womenfolk [(4)] did.*

d.   That the abuses heaped upon the people by the emigrants during their trip from Provo to Cedar City, had been constant and shameful; that they had burned fences and destroyed growing crops: *possibly knocked down fences and flattened crops (with their big herd of cattle); a call for compensation might have been appropriate, but not murder.*

e.   That at many points on the road they had poisoned the water, so that all people and stock that drank of the water became sick, and many had died from the effects of poison: *one had to be wary of alkali springs; poisoning has generally been discounted; why would they do it?*

f.   That these vile Gentiles publicly proclaimed that they had the very pistol with which the Prophet, Joseph Smith, was murdered, and had threatened to kill Brigham Young and all of the Apostles: *first seems possible as a way of riling Mormons(!); second seems unlikely en route to California.*

g.   That when in Cedar City they said they would have friends in Utah who would hang Brigham Young by the neck until he was dead, before snow fell again in the

38

Territory: *such friends would hardly survive long in Utah; an unbelievable brag?*

h.   They also said that Johnston was coming, with his army, from the East, and they were going to return from California with soldiers, as soon as possible, and would then desolate the land, and kill every d---d Mormon man, woman and child that they could find in Utah: *someone may have offered such a view to a Mormon; this was unwise, but the statement was hardly credible?*

i.   That they violated the ordinances of the town of Cedar, and had, by armed force, resisted the officers who tried to arrest them for violating the law: *if so, why didn't it appear in the Deseret News?*

j.   That after leaving Cedar City, the emigrants camped by the company, or cooperative field, just below Cedar City, and burned a large portion of the fencing, leaving the crops open to the large herds of stock in the surrounding country: *see 'd' above.*

k.   Also that they had given poisoned meat to the Corn Creek tribe of Indians, which had killed several of them, and their chief, Konosh, was on the trail of the emigrants, and would soon attack them: *poisoning not substantiated? Did the Indians unwisely eat an abandoned dead cow?*

(It seems unlikely a train indulging in such prodigious acts of criminality and wild threats, would have been waved through by the authorities in Salt Lake City who, at that very moment, were introducing a wagon train pass system. Most eyewitness accounts - but not Jacob Hamblin's post-massacre account - suggested that the Fancher-Baker Train was principally close-knit, respectable family groups, although the presence of disorderly hangers-on cannot be ruled out entirely.)

Lee continued: "Haight said that unless something was done to prevent it, the emigrants would carry out their threats and rob every one of the outlying settlements in the South, and that the whole Mormon people were liable to be butchered by the troops that the emigrants would bring back with them from California.

I (Lee) was then told that the Council had held a meeting that day, to consider the matter, and that it was decided by the authorities to arm the Indians, give them provisions and ammunition, and send them after the emigrants, and have the Indians give them a brush, and if they killed part or all of them, so much the better.

I (Lee) said, "Brother Haight, who is your authority for acting in this way?" He replied, "It is the will of all in authority. The emigrants have no pass from any one to go through the country, and they are liable to be killed as common enemies, for the country is at war now. No man has a right to go through this country without a written pass."

(In his later confessions, Lee also explained, very convincingly, why he believed that the authority Haight referred to extended all the way back to Salt Lake City. Indeed, Brigham Young's behaviour at Mountain Meadows, a year or so after the event, suggested that he, personally, viewed the emigrants as fair game. Young read the epitaph Brevet Major Carleton's soldiers had inscribed on the cedar cross above the cairn: *Vengeance is mine and I will repay saith the Lord* . Having done so, he muttered in the hearing of others present: '*Aye, and he's repaid a little*' [4]. Young also subtly encouraged his followers to destroy the cairn erected by Carleton; the cairn was soon reduced to a low heap of stones.)

* * *

Unknown to Lee, Haight was wary of the 'word of mouth'

policy guidance he had received during an earlier visit by George A Smith (one of the Twelve Apostles of the Mormon Church and the 'father of southern Utah). On Sunday, 6 September, Haight had sent an emissary to seek written confirmation from Brigham Young personally. The 600-mile return trip would normally take at least six days. (The messenger returned on Sunday, 13 September, after the massacre.)

On the evening of Thursday, 10 September, a Mormon force arrived at Hamblin's ranch near Mountain Meadows under the command of Major Higbee, counselor (staff officer cum adjutant?) to Lieutenant Colonel Haight. Higbee reiterated the policy Haight had put to Lee on 6 September. After some argument, and prayers, Higbee is said to have handed Haight's written order to Lee. The substance of the order was that the emigrants should be decoyed (Lee's word) from their stronghold, and all exterminated; no one was to be left who could tell the tale; then the authorities could say it was done by the Indians. The order was signed by Haight, as commander of the troops at Cedar City [1], but Lee was unable to produce a copy of the order at his later trials. He said that, although he personally found the plan abhorrent and said so, the majority were convinced by their fellows, who vociferously repeated Haight's list of alleged emigrant crimes. Lee felt bound to accept the majority verdict, although without enthusiasm. The emigrants' discovery of white men's involvement after the killing of Aden, greatly influenced those present. The officers' discussion, argument and prayer continued all night.

(It must be said that Lee's personal attitude to the emigrants is not evident from historic sources. While he helped spread lies after the event, he rarely expressed intemperate views in his confessions, except when rebuking the Mormon friends who later deserted him. He does not appear to have met the

Fancher-Baker party before they arrived at Mountain Meadows. After the massacre, he seems to have supported the Church view that the emigrants were a bad lot, but he said nothing bad about them in his confessions. On the contrary, he frequently commented favourably on the emigrant's courage and very obvious determination to defend their families.)

Lee [2] described how the Council broke up a little after daylight on Friday morning. All the Mormons' horses were turned out on the range, except two: one for a man to ride to overtake those who might escape; and one for Dan McFarland to ride as Adjutant, so that he could carry orders from one part of the field to another. At that point breakfast was eaten, and the brethren prepared for the work in hand.

Notes and References:

1   Deseret was the name the Mormons proposed for the new homeland they mapped out in Utah Territory. Modern day Utah includes a part of Deseret.

2.   Lee's confessions. The confessions have been very lightly edited, and some editorial comment has been included by the author.

3.   Days/Dates: September, 1857, included Friday, 11 September. This will help us to relate *dates* to *days of the week*. Some reports and witness statements are a bit vague in this respect.

4.   *Deseret News,* Wednesday, 9 September 1857: reported Nyman v. Chauncey Higbee (trial of alleged sexual offences).

5.   Brigham Young: There were several accounts of this event.

7. OUT OF THE WAY

John M Higbee

John D Lee

Illustration 7a   Militia Leaders at Mountain Meadows, 11 Sep 1857.   *SUU, jdlee.net*

This account of the massacre has been pieced together from the few eye-witness accounts which exist: principally John D Lee's confessions, but also belated statements from the other militiamen and Indians present. More poignantly, the traumatic recollections of the young survivors have been added where appropriate. Several of the survivors saw their parents killed.

Lee's written confessions [1] offer a clear but chilling description of what actually happened. To aid the reader, the confessions have been lightly edited, but without, I hope,

43

changing meaning or emphasis: for example 'Hell' in place of 'H—l'. Additional detail has been added from other sources, and (where this has been done, it is done like this, in brackets).

*   *   *

Lee wrote "Soon after breakfast Major Higbee ordered the two Indian interpreters, Carl Shirts and Nephi Johnson, to inform the Indians of the plan of operations, and to place the Indians in ambush, so that they could not be seen by the emigrants until the work of death should commence. This was done in order to make the emigrants believe that we had sent the Indians away, and that we were acting honestly and in good faith, when we agreed to protect them from the savages. The orders were obeyed, and in five minutes not an Indian could be seen on the whole Meadows. They (the Indians) secreted themselves and lay still as logs of wood, until the order was given for them to rush out and kill the women.

Major Higbee then called all the people to order, and directed me to explain the whole plan to them. I did so, explaining just how every person was expected to act during the whole performance. Major Higbee then gave the order for his men to advance. They marched to the spot agreed upon, and halted there. William Bateman was then selected to carry a flag of truce to the emigrants and demand their surrender, and I was ordered to go and make the treaty after someone had replied to our flag of truce. The emigrants had kept a white flag flying in their camp ever since they saw me cross the valley (a reference to an earlier part of Lee's confessions).

Bateman took a white flag and started for the emigrant camp. When he got about half way to the corral (wagon circle), he was met by one of the emigrants; I afterwards learned his name was Hamilton (not listed on 1990 memorial?). They talked some time, but I never knew what was said between them.

Brother Bateman returned to the command and said that the emigrants would accept our terms, and surrender as we required them to do. I was then ordered by Major Higbee to go to the corral and negotiate the treaty, and superintend the whole matter. I was again ordered to be certain and get all the arms and ammunition into the wagons. I was also to put the children and the sick and wounded in the wagons, as had been agreed upon in council. Then Major Higbee said to me: "Brother Lee, we expect you to faithfully carry out all the instructions that have been given you by our council." Samuel McMurdy and Samuel Knight were then ordered to drive their teams and follow me to the corral to haul off the children, arms, etc. The troops formed in two lines, as had been agreed upon, and were standing in that way with arms at rest, when I left them.

I walked ahead of the wagons up to the corral. When I reached there I met Mr Hamilton on the outside of the camp. He loosened the chains from some of their wagons, and moved one wagon out of the way, so that our teams could drive inside the corral and into their camp. It was then noon, or a little after. I found that the emigrants were strongly fortified; their wagons were chained to each other in a circle. In the centre was a rifle-pit, large enough to contain the entire company. This had served to shield them from the constant fire of their enemy, which had been poured into them from both sides of the valley, from a rocky range that served as a breastwork for their assailants. The valley at this point was not more than five hundred yards wide, and the emigrants had their camp near the centre of the valley. On the east and west there was a low range of rugged, rocky, mountains, affording a splendid place for the protection of the Indians and Mormons, and leaving them in comparative safety while they fired upon the emigrants. The valley at this place runs nearly due north and south.

When I entered the corral, I found the emigrants engaged in burying two men of note among them, who had died but a short time before from the effect of wounds received by them from the Indians at the time of the first attack on Tuesday morning. They wrapped the bodies up in buffalo robes, and buried them in a grave inside the corral. I was then told by some of the men that seven men were killed and seventeen others were wounded at the first attack made by the Indians, and that three of the wounded men had since died, making ten of their number killed during the siege.

As I entered the fortifications, men, women and children gathered around me in wild consternation. Some felt that the time of their happy deliverance had come, while others, though in deep distress, and all in tears, looked upon me with doubt, distrust and terror. My feelings at this time may be imagined…(Lee's first long expression of remorse and self-examination has been omitted.)… I delivered my message and told the people that they must put their arms in the wagon, so as not to arouse the animosity of the Indians. I ordered the children and wounded (emigrants), some clothing and the arms, to be put into the wagons. Their guns were mostly Kentucky rifles of the muzzle-loading style. Their ammunition was about all gone: I do not think there were twenty loads left in their whole camp. If the emigrants had had a good supply of ammunition they never would have surrendered, and I do not think we could have captured them without great loss, for they were brave men and very resolute and determined.

Just as the wagons were loaded, Dan McFarland came riding into the corral and said that Major Higbee had ordered great haste to be made, for he was afraid that the Indians would return and renew the attack before he could get the emigrants to a place of safety. I hurried up the people and started the wagons off towards Cedar City. As we went out of the corral I ordered the wagons to turn to the left, so as to leave the troops to the right of us.

Dan McFarland rode before the women and led them right up to the troops, where they still stood in open order as I left them. The women and larger children were walking ahead, as directed, and the men following them. The foremost man was about fifty yards behind the hindmost woman. The women and children were hurried right on by the troops.

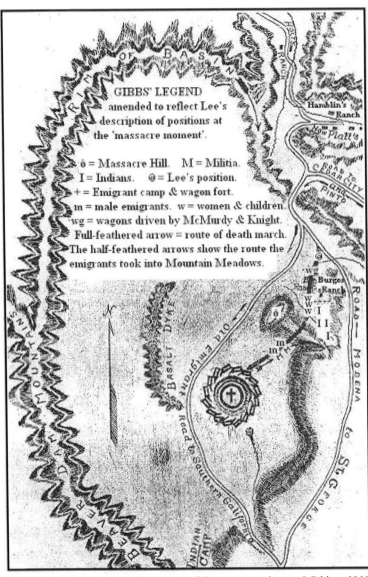

Illustration 7b   Josiah Gibbs' Map of the massacre site.   *J Gibbs, c1910*

(Gibbs' *LEGEND* has been revised by the author.)

When the men came up they cheered the soldiers as if they believed that they were acting honestly. Higbee then gave the orders for his men to form in single file and take their places as ordered before, that is, at the right of the emigrants. I saw this much, but about this time our wagons passed out of sight of the troops, over the hill. I had disobeyed orders in part by turning off as I did, for I was anxious to be out of sight of the bloody deed that I knew was to follow.

I knew that I had much to do yet that was of a cruel and unnatural character. It was my duty, with the two drivers, to kill the sick and wounded who were in the wagons, and to do so when we heard the guns of the troops fire. I was walking between the wagons; the horses were going in a fast walk, and we were fully half a mile from Major Higbee and his men, when we heard the firing. As we heard the guns, I ordered a halt and we proceeded to do our part...(lengthy remorse).

I have said that all of the small children were put into the wagons; that was wrong, for one little child, about six months old, was carried in its father's arms, and it was killed by the same bullet that entered its father's breast; it was shot through the head. I was told by Haight afterwards, that the child was killed by accident, but I cannot say whether that is a fact or not. I saw it lying dead when I returned to the place of slaughter. .

(A child survivor, Saphrina Huff [2], said she, too, was being carried by Captain Baker when he was killed; she also saw her mother fall after being shot in the head.)

When we had got out of sight, as I said before, and just as we were coming into the main road, I heard a volley of guns at the place where I knew the troops and emigrants were. Our teams were then going at a fast walk. I first heard one gun, then a volley at once followed. McMurdy and Knight stopped their teams at once, for they were ordered by Higbee, the same as I was, to help kill all the sick and wounded who were in the wagons, and to do it as soon as they heard the guns of the troops.

McMurdy was in front; his wagon was mostly loaded with the arms and small children. McMurdy and Knight got out of their wagons; each one had a rifle. McMurdy went up to Knight's wagon, where the sick and wounded were, and raising his rifle to his shoulder, said: "0 Lord, my God, receive their spirits, it is for thy Kingdom that I do this." He then shot a man who was lying with his head on another man's breast; the ball killed both men.

I also went up to the wagon, intending to do my part of the killing. I drew my pistol and cocked it, but somehow it went off prematurely, and I shot McMurdy across the thigh, my Pistol ball cutting his buck-skin pants. McMurdy turned to me and said: "Brother Lee, keep cool, you are excited; you came very near killing me. Keep cool, there is no reason for being excited." Knight then shot a man with his rifle; he shot the man in the head. Knight also brained a boy that was about fourteen years old. The boy came running up to our wagons, and Knight struck him on the head with the butt end of his gun, and crushed his skull.

(*Behind Lee's position*, out of sight, the women and children were set upon by the Indians, who recounted their deeds to Jacob Hamblin nine days later [5]:

'About a mile from the spring there are some scrub-oak bushes and tall sage growing on either side of the road and close to it. Here a large body of Indians lay in ambush, who, when the emigrants approached, fell upon them in their defenceless condition and with bows and arrows and stones and guns and knives murdered all without regard to sex or age, except a few infant children, seventeen of which have since been recovered.'

A separate observer, Hamblin's Indian boy, Albert, explained how he tried to save two young girls who had escaped and hid in some bushes; but were found:

'A man, who is an Indian doctor, also told the Indians not to kill them. The girls came out hung around him for protection, he trying to keep the Indians away. The girls were crying out loud. The Indians came up and seized the girls by their hands and dresses and pulled and pushed them away from the doctor and shot them.' *Author query*: two of the Dunlap girls? [4])

(Child survivor, Rebecca Dunlap [4], hid behind a sage bush when the massacre began; her two older sisters were killed beside her. After hearing the pathetic cries of her baby sister, Sarah, she found the infant still clutched in her dead mother's arms; a ball had shattered both bones below Sarah's right elbow. After she had seized Sarah, Rebecca was eventually reunited with a third Dunlap girl, Louisa, during the round up after the killing.)

(Child survivor, Calvin told Brevet Major Carleton [5] that he was by his mother when she was struck down; he pulled arrows out of her back until she was dead.)

Lee continued: By this time many Indians reached our wagons, and all of the sick and wounded were killed almost instantly. I saw an Indian from Cedar City, called Joe, run up to the wagon and catch a man by the hair, and raise his head up and look into his face; the man shut his eyes, and Joe shot him in the head. The Indians then examined all of the wounded in the wagons, and all of the bodies, to see if any were alive, and all that showed signs of life were at once shot through the head. I did not kill any one there, but it was an accident that kept me from it, for I fully intended to do my part of the killing, but by the time I got over the excitement of coming so near killing McMurdy, the whole of the killing of the wounded was done. There is no truth in the statement of Nephi Johnson, where he says I cut a man's throat.

Just after the wounded were all killed I saw a girl, some ten or eleven years old, running towards us, from the direction where the troops had attacked the main body of emigrants; she was covered with blood. An Indian shot her before she got within sixty yards of us. That was the last person that I saw killed on that occasion.

(At) about this time an Indian rushed to the front wagon, and grabbed a little boy, and was going to kill him. The lad got away from the Indian and ran to me, and caught me by the knees; and begged me to save him, and not let the Indian kill him. The Indian had hurt the little fellow's chin on the wagon bed, when he first caught hold of him. I told the Indian to let the boy alone. I took the child up in my arms, and put him back in the wagon, and saved his life. This little boy said his name was Charley Fancher, and that his father was Captain of the train. He was a bright boy. I afterwards adopted him, and gave him to Caroline. She kept him until Dr. Forney took all the children east. I believe that William Sloan, alias Idaho Bill, is the same boy.

After all the parties were dead, I ordered Knight to drive out on one side, and throw out the dead bodies. He did so, and threw them out of his wagon at a place about one hundred yards from the road, and then came back to where I was standing. I then ordered Knight and McMurdy to take the children that were saved alive - sixteen was the number, some say seventeen, I say sixteen* - and drive on to Hamblin's ranch. They did as I ordered them to do. Before the wagons started, Nephi Johnson came up in company with the Indians that were under his command, and Carl Shirts I think came up too, but I know that I then considered that Carl Shirts was a coward, and I afterwards made him suffer for being a coward. Several white men came up too, but I cannot tell their names, as I have forgotten who they were.

(Child survivor, Saphrina Huff [2], stated that there were originally eighteen* children gathered up, but one girl was considered too old; she saw the child shot. As Sophrina was only four at the time, Lee's final figure, sixteen, might have been correct; the seventeenth child was never recovered in the round up two years later. However, Klingensmith [3] said he, not Lee, took charge of the children, and that there were eighteen* at the start but one died - *or was she shot as Saphrina recalled?* - on the way to Hamblin's ranch.)

Lee continued:... ..(Some disclaimers from Lee omitted)...After the wagons, with the children, had started for Hamblin's ranch, I turned and walked back to where the brethren were. (...more muttering from Lee..)...While going back, to the brethren, I passed the bodies of several women. In one place I saw six or seven bodies near each other; they were stripped perfectly naked, and all of their clothing was torn from their bodies by the Indians. I walked along the line where the emigrants had been killed, and saw many bodies lying dead and naked on the field, near by where the women lay. I saw ten children; they had been killed close to each other; they were from ten to sixteen years of age. The bodies of the women and children were scattered along the ground for quite a distance before I came to where the men were killed.

I do not know how many were killed, but I thought then that there were some fifteen women, about ten children, and about forty men killed, but the statement of others that I have since talked with about the massacre, makes me think there were fully one hundred and ten killed that day on the Mountain Meadows, and the ten who had died in the corral, and young Aden killed by Stewart at Richards Springs, would make the total number one hundred and twenty-one.

When I reached the place where the dead men lay, I was told how the orders had been obeyed. Major Higbee said, "The boys have acted admirably, they took good aim, and all of the damned gentiles but two or three fell at the first fire." He said that three or four got away some distance, but the men on horses soon overtook them and cut their throats. Higbee said the Indians did their part of the work well, that it did not take over a minute to finish up when they got fairly started. I found that the first orders had been carried out to the letter.

Three of the emigrants did get away, but the Indians were put on their trail and they overtook and killed them before they reached the settlements in California. But it would take more time than I have to spare to give the details of their chase and capture. I may do so in my writings hereafter, but not now.

I found Major Higbee, Klingensmith and most of the brethren standing near where the largest number of the dead men lay. When I went up to the brethren, Major Higbee said, "We must now examine the bodies for valuables." I said I did not wish to do any such work. Higbee then said, "Well, you hold my hat and I will examine the bodies, and put what valuables I get into the hat."

The bodies were all searched by Higbee, Klingensmith and William. C. Stewart. I did hold the hat a while, but I soon got so sick that I had to give it to some other person, as I was unable to stand for a few minutes. The search resulted in getting a little money and a few watches, but there was not much money. Higbee and Klingensmith kept the property, I suppose, for I never knew what became of it, unless they did keep it. I think they kept it all.

After the dead were searched, as I have just said, the brethren were called up, and Higbee and Klingensmith, as well as myself, made speeches, and ordered the people to keep the matter a secret from the entire world. Not to tell their wives, nor their most intimate friends, and we pledged ourselves to keep everything relating to the affair a secret during life. We also took the most binding oaths to stand by each other, and to always insist that the massacre was committed by Indians alone. This was the advice of Brigham Young too, as I will show hereafter.

(When Brevet Major Carleton carried out his investigation and reported [5] to Congress in May, 1859, the oaths were adhered to, but Carleton was not fooled. From that moment, he developed a lifelong hatred of both Mormons and desert Indians. Later in his career, he was told to stop decapitating desert Indians and putting their heads on display to discourage wagon train attacks.)

Lee continued: The men were mostly ordered to camp there on the field for that night (to prevent the Indians from ransacking the wagon train; they had already been seen clambering over the wagons, eager for plunder) but Higbee and Klingensmith went with me to Hamblin's ranch, where we got something to eat, and stayed there all night. I was nearly dead for rest and sleep; in fact I had rested but little since the Saturday night before. I took my saddle-blanket and spread it on the ground soon after I had eaten my supper, and lay down on the saddle-blanket, using my saddle for a pillow, and slept soundly until next morning."

So ended Lee's account of that dreadful day, but *Jacob Hamlin's wife* described the day's tragic finale, in her (Mormon censored) statement [5] to Carleton:

"About an hour after the shooting stopped. A wagon drove up to our house, having seventeen children in it, the most of them crying. One girl about a year old, had been shot through the arm, and another girl about four years old had been wounded in the ear; their clothes were bloody.

The wagon was driven to the door by a man named Shurtz, or Shirts, a son-in-law of John D Lee. John D Lee seemed to have the distributing of the children. The little girl who was shot through the arm could not well be moved. She had two sisters, Rebecca and Louisa, one 7 the other 5, who seemed to be greatly attached to her. I persuaded Lee not to separate them, but let me have all three of them. This he finally agreed to and the children stayed with me and I nursed the wounded child until it recovered, though it has lost for ever the use of its arm.

The (next) day after the last massacre, Lee and the rest started up the road, with all the rest of the children in a wagon, and the Indians scattered off."

Notes and References:

1. Lee's confessions.
2. Saphrina Huff: *Daily Arkansas Gazette* 1 Sep 1875.
3. Klingensmith: Statement at Lee's Trial.
4. Rebecca Dunlap (Evans): *Fort Smith Elevator* 20 Aug 1897.
5. Carleton's report - but you need to be wary of Hamblin's motive at that time, and the motives of his wife and Indian boy.

8. SO MANY

Colonel William H Dame

Commander of the Iron County Militia, in southern Utah

Lt Colonel I C Haight

Dame's deputy (2IC)

Iron County officers who walked over the meadows on 12 Sep 57

Major John D Lee commander of a unit in the Iron County Militia

Illustration 8   Militia officers who toured the meadows on 12 Sep. Sources: Pg IX

Colonel William H Dame, Commander of the Iron County Militia, and his deputy, Lieutenant Colonel Isaac C Haight, visited Mountain Meadows on the morning after the massacre. Before the visit, both John Lee [1] and Phillip Klingensmith [2] had heard Dame and Haight arguing heatedly at Hamblin's ranch. The visitors were accompanied by Judge Lewis and John Lee. In his later confessions [1], Lee described the scene which greeted his superiors and their reaction to the carnage strewn about the meadows:

Lee recalled: "After breakfast we all went back in a body to the

55

Meadows, to bury the dead and take care of the property that was left there.

When we reached the Meadows we all rode up to that part of the field where the women were lying dead. The bodies of men, women and children had been stripped entirely naked, making the scene one of the most loathsome and ghastly that can be imagined.

Knowing that Dame and Haight had quarrelled at Hamblin's (ranch) that morning, I wanted to know how they would act in sight of the dead, who lay there as the result of their orders. I was greatly interested to know what Dame had to say, so I kept close to them, without appearing to be watching them.

Colonel Dame was silent for some time. He looked all over the field and was quite pale, and (he) looked uneasy and frightened. I thought then, that he was just finding out the difference between giving and executing orders for wholesale killing.

He (Dame) spoke to Haight, and said: "I must report this matter to the authorities."

"How will you report it?" said Haight.

Dame said, "I will report it just as it is."

"Yes, I suppose so, and implicate yourself with the rest?" said Haight.

"No," said Dame. "I will not implicate myself for I had nothing to do with it."

Haight then said, "That will not do, for you know a damned sight better. You ordered it done. Nothing has been done except by your orders, and it is too late in the day for you to order things done and then go back on it, and go back on the men who have carried out your orders. You cannot sow pig on me, and I will be damned if I will stand it. You are as much to blame as any one, and you know that we have done nothing except what you ordered done. I know that I have obeyed orders, and by God I will not be lied on."

Colonel Dame was much excited. He choked up, and would have gone away, but he knew Haight was a man of determination, and would not stand any foolishness. As soon as Colonel Dame could collect himself, he said:

"I did not think there were so many of them, or I would not have had anything to do with it."

I thought it was now time for me to chip in, so I (*Lee*) said: "Brethren, what is the trouble between you? It will not do for our chief men to disagree."

Haight stepped up to my side, a little in front of me, and facing Colonel Dame. He was very mad, and said: "The trouble is just this: Colonel Dame counselled and ordered me to do this thing, and now he wants to back out, and go back on me, and by God, he shall not do it. He shall not lay it all on me. He cannot do it. He must not try to do it. I will blow him to hell before he shall lay it all on me. He has got to stand up to what he did, like a little man. He knows he ordered it done, and I dare him to deny it."

Colonel Dame was perfectly cowed. He did not offer to deny it again, but said: "Isaac, I did not know there were so many of them."

"That makes no difference," said Haight, "you ordered me to do it, and you have got to stand up for your orders."

I thought it was now time to stop the fuss, for many of the young brethren were coming around. So I said: "Brethren, this is no place to talk over such a matter. You will agree when you get where you can be quiet, and talk it over."

Haight said, "There is no more to say, for he knows he ordered it done, and he has got to stand by it."

That ended the trouble between them, and I never heard of Colonel Dame denying the giving of the orders any more, until after the Church authorities concluded to offer me up for the sins of the Church.

We then went along the field, and passed by where the brethren were at work covering up the bodies. They piled the dead bodies up in heaps, in little gullies, and threw dirt over them. The bodies were only lightly covered, for the ground was hard, and the brethren did not have sufficient tools to dig with. I suppose it is true that the first rain washed the bodies all out again, but I never went back to examine whether it did or not.

We then went along the field to where the corral and camp had been, to where the wagons were standing. We found that the Indians had carried off all the wagon covers, clothing and provisions; and had emptied the feathers out of the feather-beds, and carried off all the ticks.

After the dead were covered up or buried - but it was not much of a burial - the brethren were called together, and a council was held at the emigrant camp. All the leading men made speeches; Colonel Dame, President Haight, Klingensmith, John Higbee, Hopkins and myself.

The speeches were first: thanks to God for delivering our enemies into our hands; next, thanking the brethren for their zeal in God's cause; and then the necessity of always saying the Indians did it alone, and that the Mormons had nothing to do with it. The most of the speeches, however, were in the shape of exhortations and commands to keep the whole matter secret from every one but Brigham Young. It was voted unanimously that any man who should divulge the secret, or tell who was present, or do anything that would lead to a discovery of the truth should suffer death.

The brethren then all took a most solemn oath, binding themselves under the most dreadful and awful penalties, to keep the whole matter secret from every human being, as long as they should live.

No man was to know the facts. The brethren were sworn not to talk of it among themselves, and each one swore to help kill all who proved to be traitors to the Church or people in this matter.

It was then agreed that Brigham Young should be informed of the whole matter, by some one to be selected by the Church Council, after the brethren had returned home.

Notes and References:

1. Lee's confessions.

2. Klingensmith's affidavit.

ALL WHO CAN TELL

9. ONLY IN THE DARK

Illustration 9a   Mountain Meadows: cover of *Harper's Weekly*, 13 Aug 1859

Perhaps the most inexplicable aspect of the Mountain Meadows Massacre is the Mormons' failure to properly dispose of the bodies. Apart from the gross inhumanity of their behavior at that stage, the Mormons' neglect was stupendously careless. After solemn oaths of great secrecy and some perfunctory spade work, they hurried from the scene. Although aware of the inadequacy of their burials, the Mormons seemed oblivious to the public curiosity – not to say outrage - which would follow any re-exposure of the massacre victims.

Even when re-exposure did occur the Mormons' disinterest continued, even though many militiamen would claim later that they had come to Mountain Meadows initially

61

to bury emigrants killed by Indians, not to kill emigrants themselves. No reverence at all was afforded to the murder victims until Brevet Major Carleton's detachment of federal troops arrived almost two years later.

The increasingly vile aroma which must have arisen from the meadows soon attracted packs of canine marauders. In no time at all, grisly remnants reappeared; soon afterwards the whole area was strewn with the sad remains of the hundred or so men, women and children, whose lives had ended so cruelly and so abruptly.

Illustration 9b   *Canis Lapus*: the Eurasian/American wolf.   *TOP*

Several weeks after the massacre, one of the surviving children, Rebecca Dunlap, visited the meadows with some Mormon girls. She observed animals and buzzards disturbing unburied corpses, and recognized one corpse, Jack Baker, because of his long beard [1].

Even in a remote location, there would have been the chance of discovery. Mountain Meadows was not a remote location: it was situated beside one of the busiest 'interstates' of the 1850s. Even as the massacre took place, wagons were queuing up to pass through Mountain Meadows. The Mormons managed to delay the earliest train long enough to prevent its occupants observing the annihilation of the Fancher-Baker Train. They were eventually forced to guide that train along an alternative route. Other trains were guided through the meadows in darkness, but those emigrant parties were given very strict instructions to 'look straight ahead'.

Consequently, the Mormon's guarded account of the massacre soon aroused suspicion. The manner in which many of the men had been killed - a shot in the head - was evident from the unearthed bodies; and their location - so far from the bodies of the women and children - seemed very odd to many observers. Only a few bodies appeared within, or even near the circular earthworks or central pit. What had happened? Why weren't the wagons burned by the Indians? This was a very prosperous group of emigrants: where is everything? The Mormons' explanation was rarely convincing but almost two decades would pass before their vows of secrecy weakened.

*   *   *

In May, 1859, Brevet Major James H Carleton of the US Army was sent to Mountain Meadows from California with a detachment of soldiers. He had been directed to bury the bones of the victims, the presence of which had been reported widely in California and elsewhere. In addition, he took it upon himself to investigate the circumstances of their death, and he eventually submitted a personal report to Congress [2] [3].

Carleton produced a very thorough, well-reasoned report: so thorough that, in 1902, Congress ordered a further five thousand copies of it to be produced. It is clear from the report that Carleton saw through many of the lies he was being fed by the Mormons. The picture he eventually painted of the massacre, and his identification of those responsible for it, were surprisingly accurate. Many of Carleton's findings were confirmed in John D Lee's final confessions [4].

In his report, Carleton also noted the resolution and thoroughness of the official massacre investigator, Judge Cradlebaugh, who was accompanied by Deputy Marshall Rogers and a further detachment of federal troops under Captain Reuben C Campbell.

Campbell's soldiers helped Carleton's soldiers to bury the bones. Carleton noted afterwards:

"I observed that nearly every skull had been shot through with rifle or revolver bullets. I did not see one that had been 'broken with stones'. Dr Brewer showed me one, probably of a boy of eighteen, which had been fractured and slit, doubtless by two blows of a bowie knife or other instrument of that character.

I saw several bones of what had been very small children. Dr Brewer says from what he thinks some infants were butchered. Their mothers had doubtless had these in their arms, and the same shot or blow may have deprived both of life.

The scene of the massacre, even at this late day (May 1859) was horrible to look upon. Women's hair in detached locks and masses hung to the sage bushes and was strewn over the ground in many pieces. Parts of little children's dresses and of female costume dangled from the shrubbery or lay scattered about: and among these, here and there, on every hand, for at least a mile in the direction of the road, by two miles east and west, there gleamed, bleached white by the weather, the skulls and bones of those who had suffered. A glance into the wagon when all these had been collected revealed a sight which can never be forgotten."

Under Carleton's direction, the area was tidied up; the remains were buried in batches near the place of their demise; stone cairns were erected over each burial pit to deter predators; and the area was carefully mapped. Finally, on top of the largest cairn which marked the most significant burial pit, a very large cedar wood cross was erected. Engraved upon the cross were the words: *Vengeance is mine: I will repay, saith the Lord.* Afterwards, a rude slab of granite was set against the northern base of the cairn, and two simple statements were cut into the stone:

**Here 120 men, women and children were massacred
in cold blood, early in September, 1857.
They were from Arkansas.**

Notes and References:

1. Rebecca Dunlap (Evans). *Fort Smith Elevator*, 20 Aug 1897.

2. Carleton's report.

3. Carleton's report (internet version):
   http://1857massacre.com/MMM/carlton_report.htm

4. Lee's confessions.

ALL WHO CAN TELL

10. FROM THE CRIMEA

Illustration 10   The Tithing Office in Salt Lake City.   *LDS*

Shortly before Colonel Dame and his officers left Mountain Meadows on the day after the massacre, they decided that Phillip Klingensmith - the Mormon Bishop of Cedar City - should take charge of the emigrants' property. Brigham Young would be told of the massacre, and his advice would be sought regarding final disposal of the property.

The Mountain Meadows Massacre was a cold-blooded act on the part of the Mormons. Had it been hot-blooded, like most events in the Indian Mutiny, the wagons would probably have been burned and the emigrants' bodies thrown upon them. This did not happen [1]. Everything of value was cleared from the massacre - including most clothing worn by the dead. Many of those clothes would eventually end up - still battle-damaged and blood-stained - in a cellar of the Mormons' tithing office in Salt Lake City. When their unpleasant aroma drew attention, the Mormons suggested that the clothes may have come from the Crimea [2]. Furthermore, when other items of emigrant property were disposed of in a public auction, they were described [3] as 'property taken at the siege of Sebastopol'.

John Lee offered the murdered emigrants' money to Brigham Young, the Church President, but he refused to accept it. Young directed that the emigrants' cattle be shared out amongst the poor and the Indians (the Indians were included after some prompting from John Lee). Lee was authorised to distribute both the cattle - which, by then, bore the 'crucifix' brand of the Mormon Church - and the money. Lee's subsequent actions seem to have lost him friends. The Indians gained only a few cows and a few rifles: a fact which they presented most vehemently to Brevet Major Carleton [3] as evidence of their minor role in the massacre. Carleton surmised that many of the emigrants' cattle were being sold to the United States Army commissaries to feed his soldiers.

Notwithstanding their statements to Carleton, the Indians had enjoyed 'first dip' into the emigrants' wagons, when they had leapt upon them immediately after the killing. Until they were restrained by the militia, the Indians pulled excitedly at the wagon contents, dragging out the most attractive items. Two days after the massacre, a band of Indians accompanied John Lee into Fort Harmony. It was a rather-too-obvious victory parade, which exposed the 'combined operation' which had just taken place. John Lee made a valedictory address, as the Indians whooped in triumph and jangled the tin ware held amid the bundles of pillage on their ponies [4].

Not all the property left the massacre area. Several of the surviving children suffered further trauma when they saw Mormon women wearing their mother's jewellery and clothing. Other children suffered setbacks when they tried to claim one or other of their family's belongings. To press the point, or relate the object to the massacre, was dangerous. It was rumoured that one girl who offered too strong an opinion disappeared.

The scale of the pillage was enormous: 30/50 wagons and carriages; several hundred cattle and horses (including, it appears a prize thoroughbred); a very large amount of money; rifles; clothing and household goods plus the normal pioneer equipment carried on the wagons themselves. The wagon loads could be quite varied and costly: see the *Bill of Particulars, 1848*, included as Appendix A to this section.

It is clear that, in addition to the mass murder at Mountain Meadows, there was robbery on a grand scale. Furthermore, a third crime was to follow a year or so later, when the surviving children were taken into federal care. The United States Government was invoiced by the Mormons for the board and lodging costs of the orphaned children. These charges, levied by the murderers of the orphaned children's parents, were bad enough; but Lee, at least, also charged the federal authorities for child-ransom paid to the Indians [5]. This was blatant fraud: each of the surviving children denied ever being with the Indians.

Notes and References:

1. Burning of wagons. The emigrant's wagons were whisked away from Mountain Meadows intact, but on 20 Nov 1857, in his 'official' report to Brigham Young (Utah's Superintendent of Indian Affairs), John D Lee wrote that the emigrants' "wagons and property (were) mostly committed to the flames".

2. Crimean War: This occurred in a Black Sea peninsula, 1853-6.

3. Carleton's report. (Sebastopol is a Black Sea port.)

4. Juanita Brooks. (Page 139).

5. Lee's Diary: The entry for 2 Mar 1859 noted that Lee had billed the US Government for items paid to the Indians for 'Chas' Fancher. Survivors denied ever having been with the Indians. (cited by Juanita Brooks: Page 173). See also Note 6.

6. Fraud. In Lee's 'official' report (Note 1, above), Col W H Dame appeared to be claiming several thousand dollars on account of wagons and cattle provided to various Indian bands. One might hazard a guess that these came from the emigrant train.

7. Appendix A to this section: *Bill of Particulars, 1848*

Appendix A to Section 10

BILL OF PARTICULARS, 1845

This is equipment advice for a Mormon family of five. The Fancher-Baker emigrants would probably have been equipped to more or less the same scale in 1857, but would have had canvas, rather than box covered wagons.

Major items

1 good strong wagon well covered with a light box.
2 or 3 good yoke of oxen aged between 4 and 10 years.
2 or more milk cows.
1 or more good beef cattle.
3 sheep if they can be obtained.
1000 lbs of flour or other bread, or bread stuffs in good sacks.

Food Stuff

1/2 lb   mustard
10 lb   rice for each family
1 lb   cinnamon
1/2 lb   cloves
1 doz   nutmegs
25 lbs. salt
5 lbs   saleratus (baking soda)
10 lbs   dried apples
1 bush   beans
A few lbs of dried beef or bacon
5 lbs   dried peaches
20 lbs   pumpkin
25 lbs   seed grain
1 lb   tea
5 lb   coffee
100 lb   sugar
1 lb   cayenne pepper
2 lb   black pepper
1 gal   alcohol

Other consumables

20 lbs of soap each family.
4 or 5 fish hooks and lines.
15 lbs iron and steel.
A few lbs of wrought nails.

Hardware

1 good musket or rifle for each male over 12 years old.
1 lb powder, 4 lbs lead.
1 good seine and hook for each company.
2 sets of pulley blocks and ropes to each company for crossing rivers.
From 25 to 100 lbs of farming and mechanical tools.
Cooking utensils to consist of bake kettle, frying pan, coffee pot, and tea kettle.
Tin cups, plates, knives, forks, spoons, and pans as few as will do.
A good tent and furniture to each 2 families.
Clothing/bedding for each family: not to exceed 500 lb.

Pooled Items

Ten extra teams for each company of 100 families.
One or more sets of saw or grist mill irons to each company of 100 families.

NB: In addition to the above list, horse and mule teams can be used as well as oxen. Many items of comfort and convenience will suggest themselves to a wise and provident people, and can be laid in, in season; but none should start without filling the original bill.

Source: *Nauvoo Neighbor*, October 29, 1845, and cited in B H Roberts, A Comprehensive History of the Church of Jesus Christ of Latter-day Saints, Volume 1, 539-540.

11. SLOPE SHOULDERS

Illustration 11   A charming saint.   *LDS*

By now, the reader may have formed an opinion regarding the guilt or innocence of the various Iron County Militia officers involved in the massacre. You may even have considered the role of the Mormon Church President, Brigham Young. He had delivered fiery sermons from the pulpit and, prior to the massacre, he had had many private conversations [1] with the Indians chiefs involved. Furthermore, during his later visit to the meadows, he displayed very unchristian contempt for the dead emigrants.

In the British Army we occasionally used the expression '*to slope shoulders*'. After the Mountain Meadows Massacre several militia officers sloped their shoulders. This allowed responsibility for the massacre to slip from them onto the person below them. Brigham Young did not need to slope his shoulders. In response to Lieutenant Colonel Isaac C Haight's request for written policy clarification, he had sent a letter [2] which included the sentences:

"In regard to the emigrant trains passing through our settlements, we must not interfere with them until they are first notified to keep away. You must not meddle with them. The Indians we expect will do as they please but you should try and preserve good feelings with them."

Brigham Young's response was not received until several days after the massacre, but it had been signed at Salt Lake City on 10 September: the day before the massacre. His private advice to the Iron County Militia, via his Apostle (George A Smith) may have been presented strongly enough to prompt the massacre, but Smith later denied any knowledge of the F-B train[3]. The Church President, it seems, was off the hook.

Nauvoo Legion Commander-in-Chief, Daniel H Wells, seemed to have been bypassed, or he was working with the President: so he, too, was off the hook. Responsibility passed, then, to the militia officers in Iron County. It landed on the shoulders of Colonel William H Dame, who had personally ordered the massacre. On the day after the massacre, Dame's only defence - *"I did not know there were so many"*- appeared worthless, even cowardly, to his subordinates. Dame, however, had very flexible shoulders and, as we shall see later, he duly sloped them: not once, but twice.

As part of the 'peace terms' which ended the Utah War in April 1858, the warring Mormons were granted an amnesty. The new federally appointed Governor, Alfred Cumming, was persuaded that the massacre was part of the war. Consequently, he saw no reason to conduct a lengthy state enquiry into 'that damned atrocity' [4]. He allowed Brigham Young to handle the matter within the Mormon Church.

The Church, for its own reasons, needed to conduct an enquiry. It had to placate many Mormons who had become increasingly critical of their leaders, once horrific details of the massacre began to emerge. Complaints were levelled against specific church leaders, one of whom was William H Dame. However, after prolonged deliberation, a large gathering of the church and militia hierarchy issued the following exoneration of Dame [5]:

"Parovan, August 12, 1858

We have carefully and patiently investigated the complaints made against President William H Dame, for four successive days, and are fully satisfied that his actions as a Saint, and administration as a President, have been characterized by the right spirit, and are highly creditable to his position in the priesthood and that the complaints presented before us are without foundation in truth."

This exoneration was signed by twenty-three persons, headed by George A Smith, Brigham Young's Apostle. Included among the signatories were three persons present at the massacre: *John M Higbee* (the officer overseeing the massacre with Lee) and two militiamen. Significantly, *Isaac C Haight*, too, was one of the signatories, despite his heated arguments with Dame on the day after the massacre. One can only surmise what waivers Higbee and Haight had negotiated on their own behalf. Neither *John D Lee* nor *Phillip Klingensmith* were present during the August meeting, and neither gained benefit from it.

The Mormon Church, it would seem, had closed ranks around Dame to protect him. *In the Church's eyes* [6] responsibility slipped off Dame's sloping shoulders onto *Haight, Higbee, Lee* and *Klingensmith*. Klingensmith had a relatively minor role in the massacre; and, troubled by his conscience, he eventually broke his vow of silence. Safe in Nevada, he signed an affidavit on 10 April 1871. In this affidavit, Klingensmith confessed his own part in the massacre. He said that Haight did not approve of the killing, but had strict orders from above. He also said that Lee had charge of the actual massacre and he confirmed Lee's later report of the Dame/Haight argument on the following morning.

In 1859, to further distance the Church from the massacre, several Iron County militia officers, including Haight, were relieved of their ecclesiastical duties. In 1870, as the flames of federal justice drew ever closer, both Haight and Lee were excommunicated. Four years later, *Haight* appears to have sloped his shoulders very effectively: he was re-admitted into the Church. *Lee* was becoming increasingly isolated, but *Dame* seemed to lead a charmed life. Dame escaped censure even though he personally ordered the massacre, after disregarding an earlier Iron County Council decision to rescue the trapped emigrants [7].

Notes and References:

1. *Journal of Church History* – entry for 1 Sep 1857 - cited by Juanita Brooks. (page 41)

2. Juanita Brooks. (page 63 includes all of Young's letter)

3. George A Smith affidavit 30 July 1875 (Juanita Brooks, Pg 289)

4. Principal (internet) factual reference:
    http://www.law.umkc.edu/faculty/projects/ftrials/mountainmeadows/leeaccount.html

5. Juanita Brooks. (page 169 includes a facsimile of the document)

6. The Mormon Church would eventually push Lee into the flames of justice, but hold Dame back – see next Section.

7. Richard E Turley Jr. *The Mountain Meadows Massacre. Ensign,* Sep 2007, 14-21.

12. MAY I SIT DOWN ?

The scene at Mountain Meadows on 23 March 1877.
John Doyle Lee was executed by a firing squad at
1100am: he fell back into his coffin.

John Doyle Lee
seated on his coffin

Wagons of the
firing squad

Illustration 12a   John Doyle Lee's execution.   *J Fennemore, 1877*

The federal investigation by Judge Cradlebaugh began in May
1859. A few months later, he issued arrest warrants for the
arrest of *John D Lee, Isaac C Haight*, and *John M Higbee* for
the murders. The judge also wrote a letter to President
Buchanan informing him that the massacre seemed to have
been committed *'by order of council'*. However, progress was
halted at this point. The US marshal accompanying Judge
Cradlebaugh declared his unwillingness to arrest people

without the protection of federal troops. Federal troops were not forthcoming, because they had another more pressing commitment: the American Civil War (1860-64).

There was no further progress until early 1870, when a *Utah Reporter* journalist ('Argus', aka Charles W Wandell) challenged Brigham Young's limited response to the massacre. Wandell's articles also prompted Phillip Klingensmith's very damning affidavit in April 1871. Brigham Young was unmoved and, besides, Mormon juries were very unlikely to convict any of the accused. However, in 1874 Congress passed the Poland Act [1], which redefined the jurisdiction of Utah courts: in particular, the act allowed non-Mormons to serve on juries.

Freed of the jury problem, the federal authorities issued arrest warrants for the following militiamen: *Lee, Higbee, Haight, Dame, Klingensmith*, and three others (Stewart, Wilden, and Jukes). The authorities managed to track down and arrest *Lee*; and then - rather belatedly - they arrested *Dame*. Lee seemed the easiest to convict.

Lee's first trial on 23 July 1875 – a very noisy, overtly political affair, which tried to call into question the Mormon Church's involvement – ended in a hung jury: eight Mormon and one ex-Mormon said *acquit*; three gentiles said *guilty*. The public response was predictable: a mixture of rage and hilarity. The Mormon Church suffered considerable humiliation. The federal authorities, too, were embarrassed. They got together with the Church and, eventually, set up Lee's second trial.

The second trail, which began on 14 September 1876, was very different from the first. New Mormon witnesses suddenly appeared out of rocky crevices in Utah: witnesses who pointed their fingers at John Lee. Two militiamen gave evidence: *Samuel Knight* said he watched Lee club a woman to death; and *Samuel McMurdy* said he saw Lee shoot a woman, as well as two or three of the wounded emigrants. *Jacob*

Hamblin [2] (the ranch owner at Mountain Meadows) told the court he witnessed Lee throw down a girl "and cut her throat". *Nephi Johnson,* Hamblin's young interpreter, said that Lee and Klingensmith seemed to be "engineering the whole thing".

Lee was on trial; Klingensmith was the Mormon oath-of-silence breaker. None of the witnesses could remember the name of any other Mormon involved in the massacre.

Lee faced this onslaught from his erstwhile comrades with bitterness and anger. He protested that many of the witnesses blamed him for their own foul deeds. In the end, Lee resigned himself. He instructed his attorney, William Bishop, to present no defence.

Summing up Lee's case, William Bishop suggested that *'the Mormon Church had resolved to sacrifice Lee, discarding him as of no further use.'* On 20 September 1876, the all-Mormon jury returned its verdict: John Lee was *'guilty of murder in the first degree'.* Lee refused to make a statement. Judge Boreman sentenced him to be executed three weeks later. Lee elected death by firing squad.

Lee's appeals delayed his execution. He used the three months he had left to complete his autobiography. He included within it his confessions, and prepared himself for his eventual execution. Very appropriately, this was to take place at Mountain Meadows.

Lee and his escort set off from the trial location in Beaver, Utah, in March 1877. Concealed within covered carriages and wagons, they followed the immigrant trail south and arrived in Mountain Meadows on the morning of 23 March, 1877.

Lee enjoyed breakfast at the massacre site. Later, a Methodist minister, Rev George Stokes [3], accompanied Lee to a coffin on the meadowland. Lee sat on it as his death warrant was read out by William Nelson, a US Marshal. When Nelson had finished Lee stood up and faced his audience: various federal officials; Lee's own relatives; the firing squad; a photographer (James Fennemore) tasked by Lee to produce a print for each of his three wives [4]; and about seventy invited spectators.

Lee offered his farewell and final thoughts in a prepared statement, the gist of which was:

I'm approaching death calmly; my conscience is clear before God and man. I want neither mercy, nor forgiveness. Death will be preferable to my present existence. I remain a true believer in Joseph Smith's gospel, but Brigham Young's teaching is dangerous: he will destroy the Church. I have been sacrificed by the Church; but I ask God to receive my spirit.

After shaking hands with those he could reach, Lee sat down again. Blindfolded but with his hands free, his final words were to the firing squad, hidden from view within conveniently sited covered wagons. He instructed them to aim for his heart. They did; and, as the shots rang out, Lee fell back silently into his coffin [5].

* * *

Brigham Young died five months after Lee's Execution: it is thought of appendicitis.

William Dame wriggled off the hook again. His ecclesiastical magnificence and – I presume – affable personality seems to have placed him outside the law. Despite his pivotal role in the massacre, all charges against him were dropped shortly before the second trial. This may have been a pre-condition of the Mormon Church's cooperation during that trial.

The other warrants remained extant until 1888, but no fish entered the net. Lee alone suffered punishment.

John Lee's confessions (or more fully: *Mormonism Unveiled or the Life and Confession of John D Lee*) were published in 1877, in St Louis. They became an immediate best seller, but they were viewed with scepticism by many readers. Lee, like most of the witnesses who had testified against him at his second trial, omitted to mention any personal involvement in the killing.

* * *

Lee's death was not the end of the affair. The Mountain Meadows Massacre remains a source of bitterness and resentment. In a later section of this book, I consider how closure might finally be achieved.

Notes and References:

1. <u>The Poland Act.</u> Introduced by a Vermont congressman in 1874, this act restricted the powers of Utah's probate courts, appointed a US marshal and a US attorney in place of Utah's state officials, and allowed non-Mormons to undertake jury service. A photograph of Congressman Luke P Poland appears on the next page.

Congressman Luke P Poland
of Vermont

Illustration 12b   Author of the Poland Act.

2.   <u>Jacob Hamblin.</u> According to many earlier reports, including
      his own, Hamblin was not present during the massacre!

3.   <u>Hubert Howe Bancroft.</u> *History of Utah,* 1540-1886, Ch XX

4.   <u>Ibid</u>. The wives were named as Rachel, Sarah and Emma, but
      reports elsewhere suggest that this trio were but the latest of
      Lee's nineteen wives.

5.   It was later remarked by many that God had been kinder to Lee
      than to his victims.

13. PEAKS AND TROUGHS

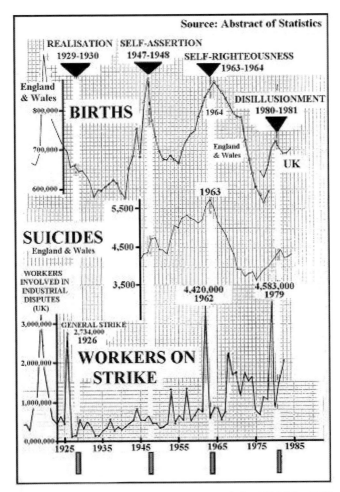

Illustration 13a   British emotion-related statistics 1925-85.   *TOP*

One of the plaques beside the 1990 (overlook) Memorial at Mountain Meadows notes rather plaintively that: *"Complex*

83

animosities and political issues intertwined with religious belief motivated the Mormons, but the exact cause and circumstances fostering the sad events that ensued over the next five days at Mountain Meadows still defy any clear or simple explanation."

I believe we can derive a clear and simple explanation for the powerful, underlying cause of the massacre. This will not excuse those responsible for the atrocity: there can be no excuse for cold-blooded murder under a flag of truce. It will, however, explain why the Mormon Church and its Militia officers behaved so badly in 1857.

Illustration 13a suggests that human emotion is tidal: peaks and troughs occur over a roughly seven to fifteen year cycle. It seems very likely that these waves of emotion are caused by the sunspot cycle. In essence, sunspot activity affects the Earth's weather; the weather - or the sunspot activity - affects human emotion. Climatic extremes are often accompanied by peaks of human emotion. These peaks of emotion seem to happen simultaneously all around the world. If emotion is peaking in Britain, it is usually peaking in Australia, USA, China, *et al.*

How do we know when the world is passing through such a peak? There seem to be many indicators: the weather is normally extreme; high profile political assassinations and terrorist incidents occur; emotion-related statistics peak; and, where conditions are favourable, social explosions occur.

The symptoms may differ about the globe: there may be assassination in USA, a social explosion in China, and a major terrorist incident in Hong Kong. Sometimes they all come at once. During the 'emotional peak' period 1987-88 (the next *Realisation*), Britain experienced a Stock Market Crash, the Great Storm, and the Pan Am 103 Lockerbie bomb. In Europe, a social explosion occurred: this led to the fall of the Berlin Wall in 1989 and, eventually, to the break up of the

Soviet Union. Had Illustration 13a been extended to the right, the already-rising statistics would have peaked.

Illustration 13a displays the peaks and troughs of emotion in Britain during the period 1925 to 1985. If we look at 1963-64, you may remember the 'indicators'. There was a spate of high profile assassinations in America: President Kennedy in 1963; Malcolm X in 1965; and Robert Kennedy and Martin Luther King in 1968. The Vietnamese President, Ngo Dinh Diem was assassinated in 1963. In Europe, at least, the weather was extreme. During the later 1960s, we saw the Cultural Revolution (Mao Tse Tung's ideological crusade) in China; and a great wave of very self-righteous social movements throughout Europe and the USA.

The four emotionally-named peaks on Illustration 13a seem to occur naturally in a repetitive cycle [1]. As we pass through the peak years, emotion elevates in intensity and a particular strong feeling is experienced by the human population, dependent upon the sequential position of that peak. To understand the Mountain Meadows Massacre, we only need to consider the *self-righteousness* peak: the other peaks are not particularly relevant. The self-righteousness peak is found about two-thirds to three-quarters of the way, in time, from an economic depression to the next most prosperous period [1]. For example: 1934 = depression; 1963/4 = self-righteousness peak; 1973 = most prosperous time.

Looking back in time, we see similar self-righteousness peaks around the following years: 1963, 1908, 1857, 1804, etc. These dates are inspired guesses based on a review of the symptoms which I have already described. You can see that 1857 is one of the *self-righteousness* peaks. (1843 = depression; 1857 = self-righteousness peak; 1867 = most prosperous time.) I selected 1857 because the 1857 Indian Mutiny [2] was an obvious *self-righteousness*-motivated, social explosion. The Mutiny was psychopathically violent and ideologically driven.

Not every country suffered a social explosion in 1857 but America certainly did: in New York. Looking back at 1857, one would expect everyone's self-righteousness to be elevated. In most cases this didn't matter, but <u>where a person was already very self-righteous that person's self-righteousness became extreme</u>. The main characteristic of an extremely self-righteous person is *extreme certainty*. Extreme certainty is also the main characteristic of a psychopath [3]. In 1857, the Mormons - who were already very self-righteous – became extremely self-righteous. Consequently, their extremely high level of *certainty* caused them to behave like psychopaths. The Mountain Meadows Massacre was an outcome of the Mormons' momentary *extreme certainty*.

Notes and References:

1.   The reason for this is too complicated to be explained properly in this short section. It is explained fully in:

THE RHYTHM OF WAR in a civilised world Terence Parker (Romans, 2007, ISBN 978-0-9554843-0-8)

2.   <u>Indian Mutiny</u>: *A very brief account of the Indian Mutiny* follows at Appendix A to this section.

3.   <u>Psychopaths</u> are unconstrained by guilt or remorse; they act without consideration of fairness, propriety, morals or the feelings of others; furthermore, they are <u>absolutely certain</u> that they have the right to behave as they do.

Appendix A to Section 13

A very brief account of the Indian Mutiny

ON THE 14TH SEPTEMBER 1857 THE BRITISH FORCE STORMED DELHI. IT WAS AFTER SUNRISE ON THAT DAY THAT THE UNDERMENTIONED PARTY ADVANCING FROM LUDLOW CASTLE IN THE FACE OF A HEAVY FIRE AND CROSSING THIS BRIDGE WHICH HAD BEEN ALMOST TOTALLY DESTROYED LODGED POWDER BAGS AGAINST AND BLEW IN THE RIGHT LEAF OF THIS GATE THUS OPENING A WAY FOR THE ASSAULTING COLUMN

This gate was stormed three days after the Mountain Meadows Massacre.

Illustration 13b   The Kashmir Gate, Delhi, India, 1999.   *TOP*

In 1600, to counter Dutch incursion into India, Queen Elizabeth granted the (British) East India Company monopoly trading rights in India. Trading posts were soon established - with the approval of local rulers - in Bombay, Madras and Calcutta: the main commodities being cotton, silks, indigo, saltpeter and tea. By 1720, 15% of Britain's imports came from India.

Almost two centuries later, the India Bill of 1784 placed the East India Company under the control of Britain's new 'Board of Trade'. In essence, Britain controlled the Company but the Company controlled - through local rulers - the areas of India it occupied. To defend those areas, the Company had its own standing army, made up of British-officered Indian units plus units of Britain's regular army – both paid for by the East India Company.

By 1857, the Company had joined up its coastal enclaves by occupying a broad swathe of Hindustan: the northern part of India. It had been able to do this by adopting a sensible strategy based upon cultural and religious tolerance. Indeed, by the mid-1800s there was a high level of racial integration – particularly with the culturally attractive Moslems. Company employees often adopted Indian dress and/or married an Indian wife; British couples gave their children Indian names, and some Company employees even converted to the Moslem faith. Furthermore, within the military units this close cultural integration allowed very close British officer/Indian soldier bonding, which minimised loyalty problems.

Unfortunately, from the 1840s onwards the British ruling classes became increasingly confident, and increasingly arrogant: not least the new wave of Christian evangelists who viewed the situation in India with undisguised horror. This and a change in the East India Company's recruiting process allowed a steady stream of haughty, self-righteous, Christian-evangelist-supporting administrators into the heart of Hindu/Moslem/Sikh India. At the same time, Islamic fundamentalist infiltration was taking place. Consequently, the wiser, older Company employees saw danger on the horizon: so much so that, in 1850, General Napier, the Commander-in-Chief of the Indian Army resigned. He had failed to convince Lord Dalhousie, his East India Company boss, of the danger ahead. Despite Napier's resignation, British arrogance continued, until the inevitable happened.

On Sunday, 10 May, 1857 - after a badly handled disciplinary incident involving cartridges lubricated with animal fat, for a new rifle – Indian soldiers rushed into Saint John's Church, Meerut, and began to murder every white man, woman and child they could find. After running out of victims, the mainly Muslim mutineers stormed off to Delhi, forty miles away, where they proclaimed Shah Zafar II – the elderly Muslim emperor occupying the Red Fort – their leader. They then began to murder all the white inhabitants of Delhi. Amongst their first victims was the family of Rev Midgeley J Jenkins, the Chaplain of the Red Fort. He was the firebrand priest who had been forcefully encouraging Christian evangelists into India: so much so, that a certain Fanny Parkes noted that '*extreme religiosity was gaining ground fast in Cawnpore*' [2]. The long term affect of this *extreme religiosity* was soon to be experienced by the British families in Cawnpore. The Cawnpore siege will be covered in more detail in the next section, but it began on 6 June and ended on 25 June. The hostages - the 200 or so women and children plus a few men - were cruelly murdered sometime in July, 1857.

The British were driven out of Delhi on 11 May, 1857, but soon gathered uncomfortably within a fortification they had created on a hill overlooking the city. It was from that base, that the reinforced British forces recaptured Delhi on 14 September, 1857 – after a battle of almost unbelievable ferocity. The cannon-ball impacts on the Kashmir Gate (see Illustration 13b) are indicative of the tumult. This attack took place just three days after the Mountain Meadows Massacre.

In due course the whole mutiny was put down, and the British Government took direct control of India, until India became independent in 1947. My wife and I toured the mutiny sites, on our own, eight years ago; everyone, at every level, was very friendly; and there was no discernible aftermath or bitterness on either side. The reason for this is explored in the next section.

Notes and References:

1. ***THE GREAT MUTINY India 1857.***
   Christopher Hibbert, Penguin Books , 1978.
   (My main reference: a very good read.)

2. ***THE LAST MUGHAL***
   The Fall of a Dynasty, Delhi, 1857.
   William Dalrymple. Bloomsbury, 2006.
   (The book covers the religious aspect of the mutiny in depth but, as the title suggests, the coverage is restricted to Delhi. See Page 61 for **Fanny Parkes's reflections**.)

14. TWO MASSACRES

Nana Sahib

Illustration 14a *Graham, c1855*

We have covered the Mountain Meadows Massacre in some detail. Let us now look, briefly, at the similar massacre which took place in Cawnpore (Kanpur), India, in June 1857.

The Indian Mutiny began in Meerut on 10 May, 1857, almost three hundred miles from Cawnpore. Cawnpore remained uneasily calm until early June. There had been surly looks, dire warnings and even some offered violence from Indian soldiers, but all had been brazened out by the garrison commander, General Sir Hugh Massey Wheeler. Wheeler was married to an Indian, spoke the language, and had spent most of his working life in India. He was convinced that the four Indian regiments in Cawnpore would remain loyal. Consequently, his contingency planning and defence preparations were minimal, despite the growing anxiety of many of his staff and their families.

Ignoring other people's advice to go elsewhere,

Wheeler prepared his 'entrenchment' (a very inadequate circle of buildings and minor earthworks) in a vulnerable position. Furthermore, it was inadequately provisioned because Wheeler believed that his situation would ease when a local Indian leader, Nana Sahib, arrived with three hundred soldiers, thought to be loyal to the British. Unfortunately, Nana Sahib nursed a pension grievance which had subdued his loyalty. Consequently, when he was approached by the mutineers, he decided to join them as their leader.

Nana Sahib's first thought was to rush off to Delhi to join forces with Shah Zaffar II, but he was persuaded to remain in Cawnpore. It was suggested that, once he had eliminated the small British force and its dependents, he could become lord of all he surveyed, rather than a mere vassal of Shah Zaffar II in Delhi.

On 6th June, Wheeler was advised by Nana Sahib that his entrenchment was about to be attacked by the three thousand or so Indians [1] surrounding him. Wheeler's own situation was dire: his inadequate entrenchment was sheltering about three hundred male soldiers and civilians, and over four hundred women and children. Wheeler was well supplied with small arms and ammunition, and even possessed some light artillery pieces, but his earthworks proved inadequate. Consequently, once hostilities commenced casualties occurred almost continuously under the mutineer's barrage of cannon-fire and musketry. Baking heat and inadequate water supply added to the considerable discomfort of the defenders.

At first, the mutineers were distracted by their pillage of abandoned British houses and the still-occupied dwellings of Anglo-Indians and Portuguese. Any person of uncertain religion or allegiance was murdered. Flames soon lit the sky above the city, adding to the worries of those in the entrenchment.

It took some time for Nana Sahib to distract his

soldiery from the delights of pillage; and even more time to focus their attention on Wheeler's Entrenchment. Much to Nana Sahib's surprise, the British were disinclined to surrender immediately to his far superior force. He ordered his cannon to move closer and placed an increasing number of musketeers in buildings overlooking the entrenchment. The musket fire and often wild artillery fire of Nana Sahib's forces wrought terrible havoc within the close packed entrenchment. Men, women and children were killed or suffered horrendous injury; at least 250 dead would be inadequately buried or thrown down a disused well before the siege ended.

A half-hearted assault was made by the mutineers on 21 June, but not pressed home. Despite this, the families struggling to survive within the few, shot-blasted buildings were increasingly weakened by deaths, serious injuries, lack of food, continuing high temperatures and a dwindling water supply. Occasional sorties were made to spike the mutineers' guns (which were soon replaced); to get a message to the British forces in Lucknow (who were themselves under siege in the Residency); and to gain intelligence, but none of this activity alleviated the suffering.

Nana Sahib, too, sought intelligence: a spy advised him of the dire conditions within the entrenchment. On 25 June, he sent General Wheeler a note: '*All those who are no way connected with the acts of Lord Dalhousie* (Governor General of India since 1848)*, and are willing to lay down their arms, shall receive safe passage to Allahabad.*'

General Wheeler's first thought was to reject the offer outright, but he was persuaded by others to negotiate better terms. Many were worried by the imminent arrival of the monsoon rains, which would soon render their position indefensible. Trenches would be flooded or destroyed and gunpowder dampened.

Wheeler agreed the following terms with Nana Sahib's

envoy: the British would hand over their position (but retain their small arms); men, women and children would be allowed safe passage to the Ganges (where they would board waiting boats to be conveyed to Allahabad).

An advance party of British soldiers was dispatched to inspect and improve the offered boats, each of which would be operated by Nana Sahib's boatmen. On 27 June, the British filed out of Wheeler's Entrenchment and walked the short distance to the Satichaura Ghat (Fishermen's Temple) beside the Ganges, where there were steps down to the waiting boats. The wounded were carried on bullock carts.

The British put aside their arms and struggled to load the boats pushed up to the narrow, over-crowded steps. Boats bottomed on the mud; others began to reveal their inadequacy. Suddenly - under the direction of one of Nana Sahib's generals, Tatya Tope - cannon were run forward from concealed positions within trees on either side of the ghat. Grape shot and ball raked the over-crowded boats. Panic ensued: boatmen began to assault their passengers, and sword-waving Indian cavalrymen rode into the shallows, slashing and stabbing at anyone within reach. General Wheeler was felled by a sword slash; men, women and children perished in great numbers amid the chaos. Many boats caught fire; others sank; but a few escaped, only to ground on nearby sandbanks. Abandoning the latter, a few survivors eventually escaped the slaughter.

As the turmoil at the ghat subsided, all the surviving men were killed. Many women and children had died in the boats, but the hundred or so survivors were kept by the Indians as hostages. They were led away to be imprisoned, with others, in the terribly overcrowded *House of Ladies* (Bibighar). Neglected, underfed and without sufficient water, the two hundred or so internees soon began to expire. As they did so Nana Sahib held a victory parade, and then began to establish his new and magnificent court. He also led celebrations to mark the elimination of Christianity from his domain. Sahib's only worry was that his hostages were dying: he directed that internees be allowed two outside walks a day, and he arranged medical attention.

Nana Sahib soon faced another problem: a large British force had set off from Allahabad, under Sir Henry Havelock, to rescue the hostages. Outnumbered by Nana Sahib's forces but professionally superior, the British force was marching swiftly toward Cawnpore, bludgeoning or outwitting its way through the Indian defences. Soon Havelock's force neared the heavily defended city which Nana Sahib and his men were preparing to defend, albeit with ebbing confidence.

Nana Sahib now viewed the hostages in a new light. He reasoned that the hostage's continuing survival was spurring on Havelock's forces. Furthermore, once they were released, the hostages would report Sahib's treachery. Sahib decided to kill the hostages but - while his Indian soldiers obediently shot a few male youths who had been interned - they refused to kill the women and children. When pressed further, the soldiers fired their muskets into the ceiling of the Bibighar.

Undeterred, even by the tearful protest of his own wives, Nana Sahib called for volunteer executioners. Five appeared: two Mohammedan butchers, two Hindu peasants and a member of his own bodyguard. After entering the Bibighar, they closed the doors behind them. Terrible screams marked the commencement of the executions, which continued for several hours: the only pause occurring when it was necessary to replace a broken blade. Early next day, the building was cleared: victims were dragged to a nearby well and cast into it - some still alive. When the well was full, the remaining bodies were carted off to the Ganges.

Sir Henry Havelock eventually defeated Nana Sahib's forces and retook Cawnpore. He placed the city in the hands of

Brigadier-General James Neil. Neil visited the Bibighar. Evidence of the atrocity was everywhere: the floor was covered in clotted blood; women and children's garments were strewn about, torn and bloodstained; and a trail of horror led past thorn bushes and trees to the well. Hair and scraps of clothing hung from the thorn bushes, and a small child's eye could be seen - still trapped in the coarse bark of a tree. Within the well itself, a sight never forgotten awaited those brave enough to peer down into the shadows.

WELL AT CAWNPOOR.—From sketch by Lieutenant Pearce, engraved in Illustrated Times.

Illustration 14b   The Bibighar and a gallows are to the rear.   *www.britishempire.co.uk*

Sir Henry Havelock had threatened to hang any enraged British soldier who looted Cawnpore or ill-treated any innocent civilian; but Havelock had gone. General Neil was less restrained: any suspected mutineer caught was first made to lick clean one square foot of the Bibighar floor; he was then humiliated in every way offered by his religion and cast; finally, he was summarily tried and hanged. Mutineers who complained were subdued by the lash. The process continued until troops had to be withdrawn to relieve other besieged garrisons elsewhere. Nana Sahib and his generals escaped, but Tatya Tope was eventually captured: he was hanged on 18 April, 1859, long after the Mutiny had ended.

* * *

On 1 November, 1858, the East India Company was abolished by Royal Proclamation. India was ruled directly by the British Government until 15 August, 1947, when partitioned India (and Pakistan) became independent.

Illustration 14c   Tatya Tope gazes down on the well at Cawnpore, 1999.   *TOP*

The Mutiny of 1857 has long been consigned to history. Within Cawnpore, both the Indians and the British have their memorials. Tatya Tope's bust gazes down upon the infamous well in what is now Nana-Rao Park, named after Nana Sahib and his brother, Bala-Rao. The British have All Soul's

Anglican Church, built on the site of Wheeler's Entrenchment. The church's interior walls are adorned with individual and regimental memorials listing the thousand or so soldiers and civilians who died in or near Cawnpore, during the Mutiny. Illustration 14d shows one of them.

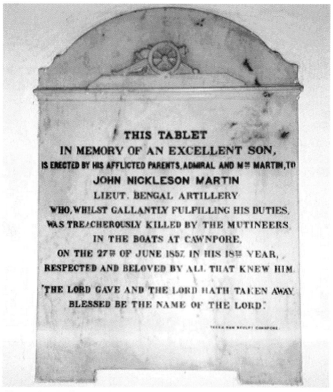

Illustration 14d   Plaque, All Soul's Church, Cawnpore.   *TOP*

The Satichaura Ghat (now renamed the Nanarao Ghat) seemed unchanged in 1999. Monkeys and goats wandered about its untidy approach; the domed temple retained its nineteenth century appearance; and smiling young Indians offered visitors a Mutiny fact sheet.

Both sides committed atrocities in 1857-58. There was a great explosion of emotion, but eventually it abated. The bereaved mourned; memorials were built; the dead were honoured, often from a considerable distance; and the mutually beneficial British-Indian relationship continued for almost a century until Independence. It continues today, and many British are still drawn to Cawnpore (Kanpur).

*   *   *

In contrast, the wounds caused by the Mountain Meadows Massacre have yet to heal. Why is this? Well, for one reason, more parties were involved: the Mormon Church, the Iron Mountain [2] Militia, the Indians, the wagon train emigrants, the survivors/relatives/descendants, and the rest of the United States.

The Mormon Church has a dark stain on its history. The Church was involved in the massacre, albeit indirectly, but has only recently tried to make amends. Despite this, the Church seems, from the internet, to regard itself as the superior agency in all matters to do with the massacre site. Until it sheds that responsibility to the United States Government, the motives and attitude of the Mormon Church will inevitably be questioned by all other parties.

Responsibility for the massacre rested eventually on the shoulders of the Iron Mountain Militia, but its senior officers sloped their shoulders very rapidly. John Doyle Lee found himself shouldering the blame and there was no one he could slide it on to. Dame, who ordered the massacre, had been protected by the Church; Haight, who had conveyed Dame's orders to Lee, successfully evaded the authorities, along with Higbee, who had initiated the massacre. In due course, Lee sat alone on his coffin and was shot. Lee's descendants feel that Lee was the Church's scapegoat. Their view seems justified.

Lee was clearly guilty of cold-blooded murder (or, at the very least, a war crime); but others were similarly guilty. Closure might be achieved by Lee's descendants, if the finger of history (or the Mormon Church) pointed to William H Dame.

The attitude of the Paiute Indian Nation is difficult to gauge, but it is clear from Illustration 14e that someone is reluctant to ascribe any guilt to the Indians. Child survivor, Calvin, who pulled arrows out of his dying mother's back, might have contradicted that view. It is clear that the Mormons' initial misinformation encouraged Indian grievance. The Indians felt they were being blamed for the massacre but gained little reward, while the Mormons escaped censure but sold off most of the pillage. Greater acceptance of the Mormon militia's pivotal role in the massacre might alleviate the Indian Nation's lingering resentment.

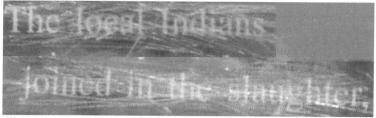

Illustration 14e   Text deletion at the 1990 Memorial   *TOP*

The wagon train emigrants – very much the wronged parties in the whole affair – lie uneasy in their meadowland graves. Wives and children are parted from their menfolk. Few of the grave sites are readily accessible to visitors and threatening notices discourage close, dutiful homage to the dead. From the moment of death the emigrants have remained at the convenience of their Mormon overlords: overlords who - at first and for some years later - sought to destroy the simple memorials erected by other, more caring individuals. That said, the State of Utah, the Mormon Church and others have greatly improved the situation during the past decade: the victims' names are, at last, on a permanent memorial.

Injustice prevailed throughout the lives of the seventeen survivors. Robbed of both their parents and their inheritance; their lives indelibly marked by unimaginable trauma; they received no recompense from the Mormon Church. Even as the young survivors departed from Utah, they suffered insults and catcalls [3] from their erstwhile captors. Their parents had been murdered as a consequence of such alleged verbal harassment. Little can be done to recompense the survivors: they are all dead. A belated, suitably abject, unequivocal apology has been called for by a few descendants. While such an apology might please the survivors' descendants and cleanse the conscience of the Mormon Church, it seems unlikely [4].

There are very many National Parks and National Monuments in the United States: each enjoys federal recognition, protection and funding. Some are large and impressive; some less so. It is very surprising that the Mountain Meadows Massacre site has escaped federal attention for so long. The massacre was a significant event, which heralded the arrival of a very violent period of American history. Fundamental moral issues were involved: natural justice, religious extremism, and the relationship between Church and State. The longevity of the controversy is testament to this. Hand-over of the massacre site to the federal authorities might finally bring about closure.

Notes and references

1. Indians. Not, perhaps, the most accurate word, but it stops me having to introduce unfamiliar ones like sepoy and sowar. It also emphasizes the event's similarity to the Mountain Meadows Massacre

2. I use 'Iron Mountain' Militia, rather than 'Iron County'
    Militia, because Mountain Meadows is now in Washington
    County, Utah.

3. Catcalls. Dr Forney (Indian Agent) - account reported in
    California's *Weekly Stockton Democrat*, 5 June 1859 –
    mentioned catcalls and 'survivor from Sebastopol and
    Waterloo (!)' taunts made at Beaver City, Utah. (Cited
    by the MM Monument Foundation on its website.)

4. Church apology. On 25 October, 2007, the Vatican, in Rome,
    finally published *Trial against the Templars* - a fourteenth century
    manuscript which absolved the Knights Templar of heresy - but
    no apology was made for the torture and execution of the wrongly
    accused knights. This is an unfortunate precedent, which shows
    that ecclesiastical conscience cleansing is not undertaken lightly.

5. Main source:

    THE GREAT MUTINY India 1857
    Christopher Hibbert, Penguin Books, 1980

6. Author's Note: I was born a day's drive from Cawnpore, and
    spent my early childhood in Meerut. My twin brother and
    sister were christened in Saint John's Church, Meerut, where
    the Indian Mutiny killings began. After the Mutiny, a rifle
    rack was incorporated into each church pew; the rifle racks
    were still there when my wife and I visited the church in 1999.

THE TWO MAIN MEMORIALS AT MOUNTAIN MEADOWS

Illustration 14f   The 1999 (renovated cairn) Memorial.   *TOP*

Illustration 14g   The 1990 (overlook) Memorial. *G&A Delange*

THE MONUMENT.

Here
120 men, women and
children were massacred in
cold blood, early in
September, 1857.
They were from Arkansas.

Illustration 14h   Carleton's cairn, c1859.   *Hutchings' California Magazine, 1860*

Epilogue

History is the chronicle of divorces between creed and deed.

Louis Fischer, writer and journalist.

Almost four months have passed, since I peered at the wheel ruts on Mountain Meadows. It is evident from the internet, that a steady procession of soldiers, historians, lawyers, story tellers and Fancher-Baker descendants had preceded me. *All Who Can Tell* is, in many ways, a concise summation of their work over the past 150 years. I hope that each of my carefully referenced extracts and illustrations honours its originator, and reminds the reader of that person's achievement.

Great drama unfolded at Mountain Meadows. A momentary whirlwind of emotion swept through Utah with disastrous consequences, leaving an untidy aftermath of injustice, guilt and remorse. The massacre and its lingering aftermath have fascinated visitors and stimulated writers. It is very likely that they will continue to do so, long into the future.

Drawing upon my own, perhaps unusual perspective of individual violence, revolution and war, I have tried to place the Mountain Meadows Massacre in context. I hope that by doing so, I have helped others to understand why such a tragic event occurred in September, 1857.

21 January, 2008   Terence Parker
Salisbury, England

Above: Author at (John D) Lees Ferry on the Colorado, 2007. Below: Ferry operation, c1875.

The Author

Terence Parker was born in India in 1939, the son of an infantry bandmaster. After short stays in the post-war devastation of London and in Warwick, his family settled in Swansea where he attended Bishop Gore Grammar School.

In 1957, after achieving top marks in the Armed Services Entrance Examination, he entered the Royal Military Academy Sandhurst. Commissioned into REME two years later, he gained an Honours Degree in Electrical Engineering before serving in a variety of appointments in the United Kingdom, Europe and North America.

While in USA, he spent two years as Chief of the Electronics Division (later Common Subjects Department) at the US Army Missile and Munitions Center and School in Huntsville, Alabama. At that time (1978-80), US high school achievement was at its nadir. His four teams of military and civilian instructors were hard pressed, but he and his family developed a lifelong affection for America and Americans.

In 1983, shortly after remote but focal involvement in the Falklands Campaign as the Equipment Manager of Army Guided Weapons, he left the Army to become an administrator at Imperial College in London. Whilst there, he decided to investigate the fundamental cause of war. He completed his purely private research in 1986: a time when few people were interested in war.

In 1989, he rejoined the Ministry of Defence as a civilian, just in time to help prepare Britain's tanks for the first Gulf War. Now retired, he has time to review his research and remember many battlefields visits: Waterloo, Ypres, Gallipoli, Shiloh, Gettysburg, the Indian Mutiny flashpoints and the banks of the Little Bighorn River, to name but a few.

This is the author's second book on individual violence, revolution and war.
An outline of his first book appears on the next three pages.

THE RHYTHM OF WAR in a civilised world Terence Parker
(Romans, 2007, ISBN 978-0-9554843-0-8)
Obtainable from the publisher (see page II) or *www.warcycle.com*

THE RHYTHM OF WAR
in a civilised world

Why do wars happen?

V. I. Lenin said that capitalism leads to war; he thought that communism could prevent war. *Sigmund Freud* disagreed: he saw man's innate aggression as the cause of war, but he thought that this aggression could be redirected into productive activity.

Who was right?

This book suggests that they were both right about the cause of war, but neither offered a full explanation. Lenin seemed to overlook the value of capitalism as a servant of civilisation and his war prevention measure - communism - has proved unsuccessful. Freud was unable to explain how individual aggression transmutes itself into a war between nations; consequently, his war prevention measure - the redirection of aggression - has yet to be implemented on a national scale.

Can we avoid war?

If we are to avoid war, we need, first, to understand the cause of war. This book reveals and explains the natural mechanism which has driven nations to war since the dawn of civilisation.

FRONT COVER (shown opposite)

Probability of War:
A modified version of
Figure 12 in THE RHYTHM OF WAR.

Photograph: Downtown Chicago, taken by the author.

Christian fresco in an Istanbul mosque.   *TOP*

We live in troubled times: Britain's small army is heavily committed in the Middle East, terrorism stalks the world, and violent pressures are building up within our towns and cities. What is going on? Will the Middle East become a second Vietnam? Will terrorism disrupt our lives for ever? Before we can answer these questions, we must understand the hidden forces which promote individual violence, revolution and war.

Imagine Charles Darwin, Sigmund Freud, General Ulysses S Grant, Nikoli Kondratieff, Gustave LeBon, Vladimir Lenin and Adam Smith seated around a table. You might ask them to discuss, agree and then explain the fundamental cause of war in 10,000 words.

Had you done so, they might well have produced this book!

THE RHYTHM OF WAR in a civilised world Terence Parker
(Romans, 2007, ISBN 978-0-9554843-0-8)
Obtainable from the publisher (see page II) or ***www.warcycle.com***